For Africa's girl child: may she find her rightful place in the social and economic development of her vibrant and gifted continent.

'The real challenge and test of the success of the Fourth World Conference on Women is what happens afterwards'
Patricia B. Licuanan
Chairperson of the UN Commission on the Status of Women

Maintaining the Momentum of Beijing

The contribution of African gender NGOs

Edited by
NANA ARABA APT
Centre for Policy Studies
University of Ghana

NAANA AGYEMANG-MENSAH
Associates in Development
Accra, Ghana

MARGARET GRIECO
The Business School
University of North London

Routledge
Taylor & Francis Group

LONDON AND NEW YORK

First published 1998 by Ashgate Publishing

Reissued 2018 by Routledge
2 Park Square, Milton Park, Abingdon, Oxon, OX14 4RN
711 Third Avenue, New York, NY 10017, USA

Routledge is an imprint of the Taylor & Francis Group, an informa business

Publisher's Note
The publisher has gone to great lengths to ensure the quality of this reprint but points out that some imperfections in the original copies may be apparent.

Disclaimer
The publisher has made every effort to trace copyright holders and welcomes correspondence from those they have been unable to contact.

A Library of Congress record exists under LC control number: 98072625

ISBN 13: 978-1-138-32430-5 (hbk)
ISBN 13: 978-0-429-45094-5 (ebk)

Contents

PART 3 CONNECTING UP WITH THE RESOURCES – A GUIDE
TO DONOR FUNDING

List of Tables

Acknowledgements

To the very many women who brought their efforts and commitment to each and every stage of producing the evidence and recommendations contained in this book, a hearty thank you for your trouble. Thanks to Ishrat Husain, Division Chief of Human Resources in the Africa Region of the World Bank for providing the support and institutional know-how on how to access resources for networking by African women – without this support, the task would indeed have been a daunting one. Thanks to the administrators of the Africa region of the World Bank who battled with a host of communication difficulties to get the monies out to the field in order to permit networking activity to proceed. Thanks also to those many NGOs who participated in bringing this work together – under-financed and over-burdened, these organisations gave of their best in setting up fora in which African women could raise their voices on development in Africa and have them recorded. Jean Louis Sarbib, Vice President of the Africa Region provided welcome and visible support for this exercise when it hit difficulties and appreciation of its products when feedback was a necessary moral tonic. Professor Paul Collier of the Centre for the Study of African Economies, University of Oxford provided support and encouragement as this hope-filled task went through its final stages. To Haddy Sey, Independent Consultant, Washington DC, who kept track of all the outputs of the networking activities and transported them to Ghana for the network workshop, our thanks. Our deepest thanks to Pat FitzGerald who by her diligence and skill brought this volume to its published form. Thanks to our children, our partners and our parents, all of whom gave support as we took the time to raise our voices in enabling the voices of others. Finally, to the Swiss Agency for Development and Cooperation Trust Fund which provided the funds to conduct the research and coordination for this book, our profound thanks.

Foreword

It gives me great pleasure to introduce this timely volume, which attests to the dynamism, resourcefulness, and resilience of women in Africa. In this collection of essays, African women, in their own voices, rightly call for development by donors and policy-makers of explicit gender strategies and protocols for the inclusion of women in all aspects of the business of development. It is a call we must all hear and heed. The Africa Region of the World Bank launched the Voices from African Women initiative before the Beijing Conference as a means to increase the influence of African women in mainstream development policy and Bank work, and we acknowledge with gratitude the financial support provided by the Swiss Agency for Development and Cooperation.

This volume should indeed help to amplify women's voices, enabling their own distinct perspectives and priorities to be heard and to shape the future direction of development policies. It also suggests ways to harness advances in information technology and communications to support gender-inclusive development. In this respect, the volume raises new challenges in the ways we think about access rights for women in Africa. The World Bank intends to be responsive. As part of the follow up to the Beijing Conference, the World Bank's Africa Region prepared a Regional Gender Action Plan, which has strengthening women's participation at all levels as one of its key strategic objectives. The Voices speaking in this volume will help to enrich this – and other – efforts and to ensure that women are truly recognised as the full actors they are in building better lives for the people of Africa. I look forward to an even richer dialogue and deeper partnership.

Jean-Louis Sarbib
Vice President for Africa
The World Bank

1 Voices and Voicing Gender Goals for Africa: Maintaining the Momentum of Beijing

MARGARET GRIECO
PROFESSOR OF ORGANISATION AND DEVELOPMENT
MANAGEMENT, UNIVERSITY OF NORTH LONDON

Voices, Voicing and Empowerment: A Move Away from the Welfare Paradigm

Beijing was the culmination of a vast amount of effort by women's organisations and women all over the world to move the debate on gender away from a simplistic focus on women's reproductive health and fertility issues to a more holistic approach on women's situation of compound disadvantage and the need for their empowerment. The scale of NGO sector activity in Beijing testified to women's unwillingness to continue to be represented through the voices of male officialdom: it was a claim for a direct voice by women in the affairs which concern them. This volume has as its goal the raising of the voices of African women in articulating and determining what the gender goals for Africa should be. The volume is not an easy read: there are often many contextual details shared by the authors in this volume which will not be shared by the readership of this volume. But those parts that we do not understand raise for us an awareness of the task that we have to undertake and the part that we have to play in gaining the knowledge necessary in order to be able to hear accurately what these African voices are saying to us.

Many of the voices in this volume protest that all to often the voices which summarise, report and record their experiences for an outside world are the voices of external experts – experts who often have failed to interact sufficiently or respectfully enough with African women to hear what they have to say and to understand their point of view. In this volume, we hear from the voices of a number of African women experts – all have standing in Africa within their own communities and specialisms and most have considerable experience external to Africa, experience which allows them to communicate with us in English. In the main, we have only edited where there was need to correct an obvious typo – the words presented here are the words of African experts all of whom are looking for substantial change in the ways in which external donors and African agencies themselves do business, most specifically in relation to gender.

The notion that the simple application of western solutions to Africa's problems will bring success has been widely discredited; the view that charity can cope with the problems of African poverty has given way to a search for sustainable projects, programmes and developments; the practice of instant experts advising on complex problems without gaining detailed knowledge of both social and economic local terrain is under scrutiny. Times are changing and the business of development has to change with them. Change is creating new opportunities for the empowerment of women in Africa: at Beijing, African women specifically stressed the need for access to the Internet and emailing facilities as a mechanism for supporting region-wide gender networking.

In the past, women – with their triple burden of child care, domestic work and employment – have experienced substantial restrictions on their travel: their constrained travel has often constrained women's opportunities for participating in decision-making. New information technologies enable even the most locally confined women to participate in communicating with an outside world: through the new information technologies women in remote locations will in the future be able to communicate their views, opinions and difficulties to decision-makers and, through electronic feedback systems, participate in decision-making processes. Currently the Dutch NGO TOOL and the Volunteers in Technical Assistance (VITA) network are preparing an extensive programme of connectivity for Africa's rural areas.

Whilst it may be some time before rural women in Africa have the opportunity to have their voices heard on the world's policy stage, women in leadership positions in Africa, whether these be positions of high political office, leadership of NGOs or academic or professional positions, can be connected electronically to the policy stage now. And African women have themselves requested that improving their connectivity be a priority – the chapter by Beth Mugo, Council for the Economic Empowerment of Women in Africa presented later in this book makes exactly that request. Voicing African women through improving their access to the means of publishing their views whether with the old physical technologies of books and journals or with the new electronic technologies of on-line information and images is a priority.

The costs of physical travel often restrict the attendance of African women at major policy meetings and professional gatherings[1] but conferences can set up electronic linkages which enable African women to enter and participate in the discourse. Similarly, conferences can schedule slots where videos are presented so that those who can not afford the attendance at important policy and professional meetings can have their voices heard. Protocols have to be developed at policy and professional meetings which ensure that those living in the less wealthy countries of the world and who can not raise the finance to attend have the opportunity to participate whether this be through the setting up of special funding arrangements by donors and professional organisations or by the setting up of routine procedures for virtual attendance. Not to ensure the presence of African women at key global policy and professional meetings is to preclude their opportunities to gain the global expert status of those frequently uninvited instant external experts whose views so often ignore the perspective of African women and whose recommendations frequently damage the interest of Africa's women.

Some agencies such as the World Bank, USAID, the UN and UNICEF have already began the process of attempting to improve the connectivity of Africa and some of this effort has resulted in the better connectedness of African women but no agency has yet established a programme which systematically targets improved communications for women. There is no programme yet designed specifically to voice Africa's women: to date there have only been projects. This volume has been possible because of one such project funded by UNICEF at the Centre for Social Policy Studies at the University of Ghana – UNICEF's resident representative in Ghana, Ken Williams, had the vision to provide email facilities to CSPS, facilities which have permitted the fast and rapid exchange of materials between authors and editors.

Linking African women leaders to the global policy environment and enabling them to link within the region also assists in the voicing of less prominent African women. Within Africa, local level women's groups have been burgeoning often without official recognition of their existence or explicit inclusion of their membership in decision-making. Winifred Chege of the Council for the Economic Empowerment of Women in Africa gives us some understanding of the scale of this movement in her chapter on East African women's networking:

> There are over 26,000 women groups with over a million members in Kenya. These groups are formed as a result of social mobilisation to address social and economic problems. They have been recognised as one of the most significant

participants in poverty alleviation in urban and rural areas. 10% of these are involved in informal savings and credit systems known as merry-go-rounds. Other key activities include agriculture and livestock by 62% of the groups, sales and services 18% of the groups, handicrafts 12.5% and social welfare.

Local and national involvement of women's groups in social and economic policy and planning is a key 'voicing' request made by African women. Enabling local women's organisations to participate in local decision-making and providing the communication and resource opportunities for local networks to link up and form national and international networks are critical steps that have to be taken if the participation initiatives of the development agencies – initiatives which are often gender blind in their construction of participation mechanisms – are to have real teeth. The women's groups of Africa, groups which are strongly linked to the provision of microfinance and credit and with labour sharing activities, represent real social capital which can usefully be harnessed in both urban and rural development but which have typically been overlooked.

The chapters of this volume are the beginning of a record of the level of social capital available for partnership with development agencies and the opening up of voices which demand that partnership as the appropriate path for African development. To benefit from these existing social capital resources, donors and policy-makers must develop explicit gender strategies and protocols for the inclusion of women in the business of development. Doing things for women – the old welfare approach – does not work: empowering women to determine what needs done and what is doable is the sustainable path forward. In this volume, highly articulate African women who are both committed and organisationally linked to grassroots women identify for us the steps that the development community and African policy-makers must take.

The discussion of gender and voices has a longish tradition in anthropology where (thanks to the efforts of Edwin and Shirley Ardener of Oxford) it has been recognised that women speaking is not enough to ensure that they will be heard. Women's voices are often disattended to or in technical terms 'muted': their messages go unlistened to until embraced by a male champion, their contributions become appropriated by their male counterparts. In order to combat the muting of women's voices there is a need to amplify both the volume of the sound and the strength of the message. The task now is to amplify the message of African women so that it is impossible not to hear it. It is the goal of this volume to move along that path.

Gender Development in Ghana: The Beijing Factor

Ghana has an active and progressive gender policy environment. Its government post-Beijing earmarked resources for microfinance for women in response to the calls from Beijing for action on that front and declared the Beijing basis of this rationale in its budget statement. This alone would make Ghana a relevant site for discussion of the ways in which the momentum of Beijing can be maintained.

Ghana has already moved an explicit discussion of the gender dimensions of agriculture into its official agricultural strategy. And indeed, given the robust work of the gender and agriculture specialist, Roseta Tetebo of the Women in Agriculture and Development unit of the Ministry of Agriculture, it is no surprise that the first Africa-wide gender and agriculture workshop was held in Ghana in 1996 under the auspices of Sasakawa (Sasakawa 2000, 1997). Ghana in conjunction with the World Bank has been involved in developing a gender strategy for development which is embodied in the country assistance strategy of the latter agency.

Women's organisations and government agencies from Ghana were heavily involved in pre-Beijing and Beijing activity and the evidence is that this momentum has not been lost: post-Beijing gender activity continues to flourish in Ghana. This is not to suggest that organisations and agencies have sufficient resources to undertake the wealth of work still necessary on gender but to indicate that whereas for many Beijing may have been just the latest UN conference, in Ghana and in Africa the galvanising impact of Beijing is still present and alive. Of course, resources are needed to feed the changes which Beijing helped activate but there is a base on which to build. Beijing generated new social capital in Africa in terms of the involvement of women in decision-making and policy activity: that capital should be preserved and built upon. Part 1 of this volume focuses upon a range of organisations, both government and non-governmental, to indicate the vibrancy and commitment of Africa's women to maintaining the momentum of Beijing. Some of the contributions are short but the standing of their authors in the Ghanaian policy environment is key: it is not the number of words which determine the significance of a statement but the ability to get those words implemented in action. All of our Ghanaian authors have been successful in doing just that.

Ghana is fortunate in having some excellent gender specialists – specialists who are often overlooked by donors in favour of external 'experts' – one such source of internal expertise is Dr Naana Agyemang-Mensah. Trained in the United States, with experience of working for the key donors including the resident mission of the World Bank in Ghana and national women's organisations such as the National Council for Women and Development and the 31st December Women's Movement, Naana provides a chapter in which she summarises the impacts, opportunities and benefits of Beijing.

A key figure in getting gender issues recognised as important in government circles in Ghana has been Dr (Mrs) Nana Konadu Agyeman Rawlings, First Lady of Ghana and President of the 31st December Women's Movement, Ghana. The First Lady of Ghana is publicly active in the support of women's issues enjoying considerable television coverage both as First Lady and as president of a major non-governmental organisation. Television is an important medium for raising consciousness around women in a context of considerable female illiteracy. The 31st December Women's Movement operates as partner to a number of development donors on a range of issues stretching from female illiteracy to transport projects. The opportunity to include a chapter from Ghana's First Lady as one of the Voices from African Women is much appreciated, speaks for itself and greatly helps in the amplification of voices from other African women. The chapter is called 'Getting the Beijing Message into the Field'; both Nana Agyeman Rawlings and the 31st December Women's Movement do precisely that.

Working on the gender strategy for Ghana from the World Bank, I was much helped by a long-standing Ghanaian expert on gender, Dr Mary Grant, the then Chairperson of the National Council for Women and Development. She stressed repeatedly the importance of obtaining better premises and better communications equipment in order to enable the National Council for Women and Development to do its work of improving the situation of women in Ghana. She was and is undoubtedly correct – the organisation which she chaired frequently encountered the Catch 22 of development, donors can pay agencies for services they provide but can not directly finance equipment or premises. Without equipment and premises, services are hard to provide and gender organisations are forced to be more 'voice' than 'activity'. Despite the constraints, it faced the NCWD kept a constant, visible and robust message on gender at the front of Ghana's policy. Dr Mary Grant took that message to Beijing and repeats it here in her chapter entitled 'Gender Goals of the Immediate Past'.

In the next chapter, two of Ghana's gender experts, Professor Nana Araba Apt and Dr Naana Agyemang-Mensah, combine their efforts to provide us with 'An overview of Ghanaian gender activity'. This chapter gives us a sound indication of the level of gender activities in Ghana and provides a local overview of what is going on as opposed to the 'external expert' vision which often misses the depth and form of local gender development.

Ghana has a long history of women's involvement in trading and the Ghanaian Association of Women Entrepreneurs provides us with a chapter which both reflects that history and updates women's entrepreneurial activities into the modern period. In 'Enterprising Women: the Business of Building Women's Economic Networks' Lucia Quakye reports on a major international forum of women entrepreneurs held in Ghana post-Beijing and conveys the key messages and recommendations emerging from that event.

Legislation affecting women's rights to control over their own bodies, custody of children, entitlement to property and employment rights varies across Africa. Within Ghana, both government and women's organisations have worked towards improving the legal status of women and ensuring that where legal progress is achieved this is translated into customary practices as well. FIDA Ghana, an association of women lawyers, has played a critical role in this process in Ghana. Mrs Rebecca Osei-Boateng, Administrator, FIDA Ghana, provides us with a chapter 'Leading the Legal Battle: Gender Rights in Ghana' which records this history.

Nana Araba Apt and Naana Agyemang Mensah combine forces once again to provide a final chapter on the need to develop communications linkages and databases which permit African women to join together in developing coherent gender strategies for Africa. Nana Araba Apt has already developed a web site at the Centre for Social Policy Studies in Ghana and with Naana Agyemang Mensah explores the ways in which that web site could be used more fully to the benefit of African women's organisations in a chapter entitled 'Keeping Connected and Moving Forward: the Importance of New Technology'.

The Voices from African Women Initiative: Listening at the World Bank

Beijing was already set to be the venue for a large NGO gender presence and an important forum for gender activities when I joined the World Bank as Social Scientist, Gender Team in the Africa Region in June 1995. Recognising that whilst much had been done to ensure a World Bank organisational presence at Beijing, it was clear that there was still space for some regional action for that particular meeting. African women had met previously in Dakar[2] to put together an African Platform for Action, a well organised and important initiative, and it was clear that the appropriate way of having a regional presence at Beijing was through the funding of African participation at the meeting and the funding of post Beijing network activities in Africa thereafter.

The Swiss Agency for Development and Cooperation Trust fund generously permitted the conversion of existing trust monies into a Voices from African Women Initiative to support African attendance at Beijing and post-Beijing activities in Africa. Managers in the Africa region of the World Bank lent their support to the initiative and despite the many logistical difficulties in setting up such an initiative, and with the great assistance of departmental administrators and secretaries, the initiative was up and running in time to fund the attendance of Winifred Chege from the Council for the Economic Empowerment of Women in Africa (CEEWA) at Beijing.

The logic behind the initiative was that African women should play the key role in identifying priorities and possible courses of future development action in respect of gender in Africa. The object was to find the resources and create the space to hear the voices of African women – a group which frequently has been poorly represented at the policy table. It seemed the most effective and practical way forward lay in networking: from the Africa region, we started to search for African women who were active in the various areas of the African Platform for Action and who would themselves be resourced through the Bank funding to undertake networking within their region on their specific areas of expertise.

There were many obstacles to the development of this model of gender activity: the way in which the Bank normally did business focused more upon the production of a product such as a report rather than focusing upon the development and resourcing of networks of relationships and some sticky moments were experienced in advancing this relatively new approach. But in writing the terms of the project in order to get Trust Fund approval, I had been advised by an old hand to specify that it would be appropriate to indicate explicitly that the resources would be dispersed in Africa and in such a way as to minimise any difficulties African women might have in gaining access to these funds. Through a process of consulting with African NGOs and outreaching through African organisations, a process which reached deep into the African bush in respect of our agricultural expert, six African women took on the job of networking upon six areas of action relevant to the African Platform for Action. Each woman was resourced for networking to the tune of $3,000 and was paid a consultancy fee to produce a report, tape or video recording that networking process. As the organisation learned this new mode of doing business, there were occasional hiccoughs but with a lot of administrative and management support, the contracts went out to the various parts of Africa, the payments were made in the various resident missions and the reports, videos and tapes came back in a timely and educative form. The Bank's organisational structure had undoubtedly helped the process forward and the next stage of assisting in the voicing African women and bringing their voices to the policy stage had already been planned for.

One year after Beijing it had been decided, and in response to African requests, a post-Beijing African meeting would be held in which these networkers could bring their information one to another, synthesise the materials and prepare the materials for dissemination to a wider audience. The meeting was organised by Professor Nana Araba Apt, Chair of the Department of Sociology at the University of Ghana in collaboration with the World Bank and took place in Ghana at the Centre for Social Policy Studies (a UNICEF supported centre). The meeting was facilitated by Dr Naana Agyemang-Mensah, who played a key role in preparing Ghana's gender delegation to Beijing – with great skill, Naana brought the meeting to the successful identification of recommendations to be forwarded to the World Bank, other key donors and to be broadcast on the World Wide Web. These recommendations are included as the next chapter of this book.

The post-Beijing meeting was entitled 'Voices from African Women: Experts in our own development – participants in our future' and at the meeting the key networkers were joined by over 27 participants from other organisations. The proceedings were filmed and converted into an advocacy tape for distribution to grassroots organisations and donors by the Centre for Social Policy Studies. The availability of a tape allows the voices of the women on this initiative to be directly heard in distant locations – locations which many do not have the resources to travel to and locations where donors have been relatively slow to bring them to. The tape has been watched by a number of senior personnel in donor agencies including Jean Louis Sarbib, Vice President of the Africa Region – it is a new mode of advocacy and information which enables those with busy schedules to make the time to listen.

The contributions of the Voices from African Women networkers are presented here as separate chapters in the second part of this book. Each addresses a different theme linked to the African Platform for Action, to the calls of Beijing and to the on-the-ground gender goals of Africa's women. Africa's special and distinctive cause in Beijing was that of the girl child. Nana Araba Apt networked with women and children in the rural and urban areas of Ghana to produce both a chapter and a video on 'education and the girl child'. The Right Honourable Madame Aïcha Bah, Minister of Pre-University Education and Vocational Training, Guinea and a member of the

Forum of African Women on Education has provided us with a chapter on 'Gender and Access to Education' which describes the situation in Guinea and outlines the activities of the government of Guinea and FAWE to improve the educational situation of Africa's girl child. Madame Aïcha Bah's chapter provides us with good and concrete guidance on the moves that can be made to improve the lot of Africa's girl child immediately.

The role of women farmers in Africa has been much neglected with very negative consequences for agricultural productivity and growth and for household food security. Using outreach techniques, the Voices from African Women initiative made contact with a gender and agriculture project worker in rural Nigeria – quite an achievement from World Bank headquarters in DC and even more of an achievement on the part of the gender and agricultural specialist who had to overcome major communication obstacles even to accept the contract. Esther Susuyu Mbanyiman had to overcome more than one set of communication and logistic difficulties to place her voice and the voices of those whom she consulted and represented on the record. Her chapter on gender and agriculture in Nigeria provides many suggestions on how development policy and practice can be improved in this area.

The Honourable Miria Matembe, a respected gender activist and distinguished parliamentarian, raises her voice in this volume in the cause of the political empowerment of women. Matembe was in fact the inspiration for the Voices from African Women initiative: at a USAID meeting on the need for gender issues to be explicitly addressed in Africa, Matembe had called the attention of the room to the need for post-Beijing policy meetings to be held in Africa in order to enable African women to attend them and make contact with one another in order to form viable gender goals. It was in response to this public call for such a meeting that the workshop was called. With resources from the Voices From African Women initiative, Miria Matembe networked with Uganda women on the issue of political empowerment and in addition networked with and made a video of senior African women pressing the cause of the greater political empowerment of African women.

Beth Mugo, a leading Kenyan businesswoman and politician, uses her voice to stress the importance of the economic empowerment of women. Successful in her own right – she is given as a leading entrepreneurial example in the recent World Bank publication, 'African Management in the 90s' by Mamadou Dia – she is Chairperson of the Council for the Economic Empowerment of Women in Africa and provides a strong role model for woman entrepreneurs as well as an active advocate of the economic rights of women with the least resources in the society. Her chapter on the necessity of the economic empowerment of women is an excellent example of the movement away from welfare discourses around women's needs towards an empowerment discourse on how to remove the obstacles to women's success and survival.

Dr Pauline Biyong is a highly respected development consultant and Chairperson of the African Poverty Reduction Network, a network which advises the World Bank on poverty alleviation in Africa. Pauline networked on urban development and women's organisation in Cameroon. Her primary contribution was a video in French of low income women talking about the infrastructural and practical difficulties they face living in the urban areas of Cameroon. The text of the video has been translated into English and is produced here as a chapter – the video contains many graphic images which this text is now silent on but in the future it may be possible to find an arrangement whereby text and video are packaged together for distribution through the normal book retail system.

Winifred Chege, Federation of Grassroots Women's Association, Kenya and the Council for the Economic Empowerment of Women in Africa, used her networking resources to collect information and raise consciousness on grassroots women's involvement in poverty alleviation in East Africa. On the basis of a three month dialogue with women's groups in Uganda, Namibia, Ethiopia and Kenya, a dialogue which involved a network of researchers as well as respondents, Winifred Chege has authored a chapter which describes the activities of grassroots women in attempts to alleviate their own poverty and makes recommendations on what policy-makers can do to assist them in their goal.

In addition to the meeting held at CSPS, University of Ghana, resources from the Voices from African Women Initiative were used to finance a West African regional workshop of the Council for the Economic Empowerment of Women in Africa which was organised by Lorraine Osei Mensah of the Credit Union Association. It was the first West African regional meeting of the Council and was a tribute to the organisational skills of Lorraine and her colleagues. In line with the intentions of the funders and the project task manager, the budget for the workshop was transferred completely to the local agency with the instructions to the local Bank office that minimal bureaucracy should attend the disbursement of funds. In her chapter, Lorraine reports on the meeting: it provides us with the type of local information that those responsible for shaping credit policy rarely consider or have at their finger tips. Gender and microfinance has been a much neglected area in development policy and there continues to be a considerable gap in the resources designated for this activity as compared with the demand for such services: similarly, there seems to be a dearth of professional training or education in this area. Microfinance is an issue on which African women have raised their voices but the policy response is still slow in coming.

Connecting Up with the Resources

By the end of Part 2, our African voices have raised a number of clear and concrete messages for our hearing. The goal must now be to deliver these messages to policy-makers for implementation. The third part of this volume investigates the ways in which African NGOs can connect up with donor agencies through the new information technologies. Electronic lobbying and electronic advocacy have already begun in the field of development, in some cases with donor support and in some cases independent of such support.

Major aid donors are already involved in setting up home pages and electronic interactive sites. Electronic modes offer more open network opportunities for local organisations attempting to link up with international organisations. 'Smart' or 'intelligent' funding applications may not be very far away: direct home banking has a parallel use in development banking – NGOs funded through 'intelligent' administration could strip away layers of the unnecessary bureaucracy which develops with the presence of donor field personnel who do not have the necessary authority to resource projects.

Taking each of the lead donors in turn, information is provided on how to access the relevant web sites, email addresses and lobbying campaigns relevant to gaining access to resources from that donor.

We end the book with an epilogue by Margaret Grieco and Stephen Denning, Director of Knowledge Management at the World Bank which looks at ways in which donors can better harness the new technology to promote the gender goals of Africa as identified by African women and so maintain the momentum of Beijing.

Notes

1   At the World Conference on Transport Research in Sydney in 1995 there was but one African woman present despite the importance of women in the transport structure of Africa Two years later and post-Beijing at the World Congress on Gerontology, also held in Australia, there was once again only one black African woman present.

2   The African Platform for Action was developed to ensure that the voices of African women received adequate attention and representation at the fourth World Women's Conference held in Beijing in September 1995. The African Platform for Action is a synthesis of regional perspectives and priorities which provides a framework for action in the formulation of policies and implementation of sustainable programmes for the advancement of women. The Platform was developed at the fifth African Regional Preparatory Conference to Beijing on Women held in Dakar, Senegal in 1994. The Platform for Action aims to accelerate the social, economic and political empowerment of women at all stages of their lives. It articulates indigenous African gender priorities and identifies critical areas of concern.

Reference

Sasakawa 2000 (1997), *Women, agricultural intensification and household food security*, Sasakawa 2000: Mexico.

2 The Gender Goals of African Women: Recommendations from the Voices from African Women Network

VOICES FROM AFRICAN WOMEN WORKSHOP

Introduction

The Voices from African Women initiative was promoted by the World Bank as a means of amplifying the voices of African women on key gender issues upon the African continent – the initiative was financed by the Swiss Trust Fund and administered by the World Bank. Six African women held contracts to network within Africa on key gender issues. These networkers were involved in organising conferences and facilitating gender networking within the region. This networking activity culminated in an Africa-wide workshop of over 27 participants of African organisations, both governmental and NGOs and the whole of these proceedings was videoed and edited into a video tape which can used for advocacy on African gender issues. It is a way of bringing the voices of African women into the centre of the policy stage: resource constraints frequently prevent their actual presence, film provides a means by which their voices and experience can be relayed accurately and authentically.

The participants met on the last day of the workshop to draft recommendations to be advanced to the Vice Presidents of the Africa region of the World Bank and to all policy interests and agencies relevant to gender change in Africa. These are their recommendations.

General Recommendations

- There is a need to utilise African women experts on African issues.
- Strengthen the Voices from African Women network to monitor and evaluate both national and global plans of action in respect of women.
- Strengthen and resource African women's organisations and networks.
- Work to promote transparency and accountability of donor agencies.
- African women should provide support for each other in times of need.
- The World Bank should support its policy statements with tangible actions e.g. the appointment of an African woman as the gender coordinator of the African region.

Economic Empowerment of Women

Macro-level

- Development of gender and culture sensitive economic models.
- Encourage women's participation and representation in economic and political structures.
- Enhance women's ability to lobby.
- Resource women so as to enable them to identify relevant structures for lobbying and participation.
- Analyse national budgets in respect of gender components.
- Lobby to reduce moves towards the total liberalisation and globalisation of our economies at the global and national level.
- Ensure gender disaggregation of data.
- Develop a research initiative on gender and economic issues.
- Develop an appropriate quantification of women's work.
- Lobby for the conversion of forgiven debt into social expenditure on gender.

Micro-level

- Improvement of infrastructural facilities for storage and marketing.
- Development of labour saving and other appropriate technologies which are gender friendly.
- Initiatives through which women can improve their contribution (to economic development) should be measurable.

- More support should be given to food crops which have an immediate impact on women.
- Need to develop policies designed to improve women's incomes.
- Need for economic literacy, information and skills training for women.
- Linkages between micro and macro to be identified by experts who should work to bridge the gap.
- Need for special credit institutions and systems to target women with attention to grassroot women's needs.
- Need for (gender) monitoring mechanisms to key in on implementation plans and policies.

Urban Development and Women's Organisation

- Promote women's access to potable water, housing and transportation.
- Improvements in women's access to health care provision with a specific focus on accessibility and affordability.
- Promote women's access to resources for economic activities.
- Improve local trading laws to become women friendly.
- Pay attention to the needs of women and other vulnerable groups in urban areas.
- Improve women's access to information, education and communication training in the urban sector.
- Lobby for the recognition of the importance of the informal sector.
- Strengthen existing women's organisations and encourage their formation in areas where they do not exist.
- Build upon existing indigenous African financial and entrepreneurial structures which have been successful.
- Lobby in respect of obtaining a share of CGAP (and other microfinance resources) for the poor of Africa – Africa's women.
- Recognise African women's networks and organisations and utilise the expertise of African women on expert groups set up to work on African affairs.

Women and Agriculture

- Improve rural infrastructure for the distribution of the agricultural produce of women.

- Support and sponsor women's participation in policy formulating institutions at all levels of government.
- Promote awareness campaign for men and women on the disadvantages of the gender division of labour.
- Promote financial and technical support for agriculture and development in female-headed households.
- Identify and promote location-specific labour saving technology for women.
- Support awareness campaign among rural women to inform them about their rights under existing laws.
- Improve women's access to and control of land, technology and credit.
- Improve women's access to agricultural inputs.
- Support education and programmes aimed at sensitising people against negative sociocultural practices which constrain the advancement of women in agriculture.
- Promote the establishment of agro-processing industries to forestall harvest losses.
- Diversify agricultural production.
- Encourage indigenous food crop production and promote their export.
- Guarantee women's control over cash incomes derived from agricultural production.
- Promote the availability of agricultural incentives to improve food security.
- Institute mechanisms for appropriate pricing for agricultural produce both nationally and internationally.

Education and the Girl Child

- Identify the relationship between poverty and girls' education and recognise the importance of girls' incomes to family survival and boys' education.
- Recognise the constraints that school fees place on the education of girls.
- Provide bursaries and scholarships for girls' education, most particularly within poor communities.
- Recognise the irrelevance of the present school curriculum and methodology to the life needs of the majority of girls.
- Recognise the inadequacy of existing facilities and resources for girls' education.

- Recognise the role that pregnancy plays in girls dropping out of school.
- Develop information, education and communication campaigns to create awareness about the importance of girls' education.
- Establish personal development programmes for girls e.g. self esteem, assertiveness, etc.
- Facilitate the return of teenage mothers to school.
- Develop curriculum, teaching methods and timing of education to be sensitive to the needs of girls.
- Devise innovative ways of preventing and legislating against child marriage e.g. raise the legal age of marriage and ensure that marriage is with the consent of both parties.
- Integrate the disabled into regular schools to facilitate the education of the physically and visually challenged.
- Reform the socialisation of boys and girls into gender roles.
- Provide vocational education and schools for girls.
- Provide literacy programmes at all stages of women's and girls' lives.
- Encourage the establishment of support systems for teenage mothers.
- Take schools closer to girls and provide needed resources e.g. female sanitary towels, women-positive educational materials, etc.
- Develop labour saving devices to ease women's burden so girls can go to school.

Political Empowerment of Women

- African women suggest their involvement in peace missions and other structures which have been established for conflict resolution.
- Establishment and strengthening of national machineries for the advancement of women and application of affirmative action.
- Transformation of existing political structures and systems to make them women friendly.
- Gender sensitisation of the society by working to demystify the role played by men and boys in society.
- Promote women who have become successful in politics as role models so as to motivate other women to participate in politics.
- Establishment of training centres for political and economic skills development.
- Establishment of systems of fund raising to support women politicians financially.

- Assist women to develop a specific political agenda and broaden networks and build alliances both nationally and internationally.
- Political awareness creation and political skills development for grassroots women to enable them to participate in voting and contesting for local councils.
- Encourage women to use the mass media to increase women's political participation.
- Support constitutional reform in order to remove discrimination against women.

These recommendations are advanced in order to maintain the momentum of Beijing in developing more appropriate gendered economic and social policies for Africa.

Voices from African Women workshop
Accra, Ghana
September 1996

PART 1
GENDER DEVELOPMENT IN GHANA: THE BEIJING FACTOR

3   Impact and Opportunities: The Benefits of Beijing

DR NAANA AGYEMANG-MENSAH
GENDER AND DEVELOPMENT CONSULTANT AND
COORDINATOR, ASSOCIATES IN DEVELOPMENT, GHANA

Consolidating the Home Front

The process of preparing towards the Fourth World Conference was a hectic one. Several activities were held at national, regional and international levels to provide opportunities for women to mobilise, learn, share experiences and to lobby one another for support.

In the Africa sub-region meetings were held to identify critical needs, as a prelude to the preparation of the African Platform for Action which was finalised at the Regional Meeting in Dakar in 1994. Here in Ghana two major Regional Preparatory Meetings were held:

- a Consensus Building Meeting which preceded the Africa Regional Meeting; and
- a Strategy Formulation Consultative Meeting, which was held shortly before the World Conference.

The Accra Consultative Meeting and the Addis Ababa Meeting in July 1995 were not only unique in their focus on consolidating African women's position on the Critical Areas of Concern in the Global Platform for Action which were still pending debate in Beijing, but also in their ability to strengthen the solidarity among sister countries, and to establish permanent networking relations. The result was a well prepared and determined team of African delegates with a common sense of purpose.

Beijing: The Experience and the Substance

Beijing offered women from all walks of life a rare opportunity to meet, talk, learn more about themselves, and defend those rights which belong to them. Women affirmed their full citizenship in the world, and raised the awareness of the world to the outstanding debts owed to women, and the need for policies and commitments to repay those debts. They highlighted the unequal relationship between men and women, and proposed comprehensive strategies to effect positive changes in women's situation. They provided hard facts from their experiences, to prove that while women's issues have always been treated as separate and lesser than the primary agendas of governments, women's issues are not only global issues, but primary agendas which are necessary for the achievement of human progress. The conference established that development cannot be adequately addressed without rectifying imbalances in the talents and strengths of men and women and eliminating women's social exclusion, marginalisation and discrimination.

Perhaps the greatest impact of the Conference was the acknowledgement of the universality of women's problems across the globe, and of African women's slow pace of progress in the quest for social, economic and political emancipation. Some of the critical issues which sunk in as areas requiring analysis and action by women as they left Beijing to take leadership in the implementation of the Platform for Action in their various countries were as follows.

Political Participation and Decision-making

Exposure to the outstanding performance of females in leadership and policy-making roles in their countries stressed the fact that the creation of sustainable, economically developing democracies, rests upon the extent to which women, and not just men, gain equal access and opportunity to exercise choices in the political sphere.

The invisibility of women from positions of power and decision-making in most countries was acknowledged with dismay as a major factor in the marginalisation of their issues. The need therefore for women to increase their ascendancy to positions of authority within the public sector and within parliament was emphasised. African women politicians urged others to remove the constraints and obstacles to their political activism and take advantage of the emerging opportunities. The need to tap the power of parliamentarians to change the parliamentary culture to make it more 'woman-friendly' by ensuring that members of parliament are well informed about women's issues, and that the latter are made their priority issues, was urged.

Poverty Alleviation

Practitioners and researchers shared field experiences which highlighted some of the problems which the women face as a result of development policies and practices which are put in place without consultation with the women supposed to be the beneficiaries. While women were noted to be the poorest of the poor, it was also ironically revealed that merely closing gaps does not translate into improvements in women's situation, since in some cases economic improvements in the labour markets may lead to more miserable situations for women, where such improvements result in unfavourable competition for women, who are often without the requisite education, or where those who may have the education find it difficult to combine outside work with the domestic workloads.

The Girl Child

The unique importance of a girl's childhood opportunities to her future life as a woman was underscored in relevant discussions.

Education

The catalytic effect which girls' education has on every dimension of their development was highlighted. The need to ensure that investments in education are augmented by investments in other areas such as nutrition, immunisation, safe water and sanitation, child care, which factors go to safeguard the well being of children so that they can take full advantage of educational investments was noted. The role of education in opening up leadership and decision-making positions for women was also underscored.

Peace

The special role that women can play in maintaining national and international peace was emphasised especially, since it is they and their children who suffer most from the effects of war. The need to ensure that human security takes priority over state security which has traditionally been defended by citizens and the force of arms was emphasised. The importance of advocacy and a reorganisation of national spending to disfavour military spending were emphasised.

Health

Sub-Saharan Africa's situation as the only region where women's health has deteriorated was highlighted and women were urged to devise strategies to protect themselves from physical, sexual and psychological ill-health, particularly that which derives from violence.

Violence against women was well highlighted especially during the NGO forum, as an often disregarded but significant source of women's subordination, lack of self-confidence and seeming apathy. The need for women to stand up to their abusers was stressed as the only way out of oppression.

Role of the Media

The way in which the media is used to discredit women was cited as the same through which it can be positively employed to enhance women's image. The importance of ensuring that women participate as influential players in the media sector was mooted as a potentially powerful way of improving general awareness about women's contributions towards societal development.

Facing the Challenge Back Home

According to the Chairperson of the UN Commission on the Status of Women, Patricia B. Licuanan, 'the real challenge and test of the success of the Fourth World Conference on Women, is what happens afterwards'. Beijing did not only give women the opportunity to see that their problems are universal be they in the North or in the South, but it also provided for women, a rude awakening to their need to mobilise for action which results in tangible improvements in their lives. Awareness was raised to the fact that the majority of women are victims in fundamental ways which constrain their talents and strengths and must now work on changing themselves, their households, their institutions and the societies which they help to build. Women have realised that their right to respect and dignity will only be changed by women themselves.

Now that the stampede of Beijing has ended and the dust has settled, action is needed to actualise what was begun at home and forged in Beijing, to their logical conclusions. A vision of justice and opportunity for all women needs to be realised and that is the challenge that should unite all women for action.

Back here in Ghana, innovative steps towards the implementation of the Platform have been initiated to inform and sensitise policy-makers and the public at large to the issues discussed in Beijing, to evolve new strategies to reduce women's poverty through targeted actions such as mobilising for a Women's Bank, to review national priorities and evolve concrete action plans: while a Memorandum, proposing Affirmative Action to enhance women's access to decision-making positions and sociopolitical participation has been submitted to, and accepted by government, in principle. The government has instituted measures to increase girls' access to education and has recently announced plans to review the Health Ministry's Cash and Carry system which has made it difficult for many poor women to access health care for themselves and their children.

While these actions are plausible, it must be stressed that the effective promotion of women's advancement will depend on the extent to which necessary changes are effected in the social attitudes, beliefs, values and practices of the persons and the institutions whose responsibility it is to actualise the implementation of the laudable policies and programmes aimed at implementing the Platform for Action.

Women are victims in most fundamental ways which hinder their talents and strengths from being tapped for development. Invisible barriers of attitudes and biases hinder women's advancement to positions of power and decision-making, and the influence of socialisation and conformism work to maintain the status quo. Society should no longer be allowed to hide behind custom and culture to deny women their *Human Rights*. Women need to look for the reasons that justify persistent disparities between men and women in terms of social expectations and prescriptions, as well as in decision-making authority and control over themselves and what is theirs. Obstructive cultural attitudes and biases need to change and so should those situations where oppressive power relations govern the lives of men and women.

Women must now work on changing themselves, their households, their institutions and the societies which they help to build. Article 5 of the 1979 Convention on the Elimination of All Forms of Discrimination Against Women calls for 'the modification of social and cultural patterns, sex roles and the stereotyping that are based on the idea of the inferiority or superiority of either sex'. The need for massive changes in attitudes, beliefs, practices and stereotypes can not be stressed enough. It is important to recognise the unequal relationship between men and women and work on evolving comprehensive strategies to effect positive changes in women's situation.

In the area of *education*, as special efforts are put in place to ease girls' access to education, we need to ensure that investments are not wasted and that school pupils stay in school long enough to be able to utilise their education profitably. We need therefore to take action for instance about the cultural practice of early betrothal and child marriage, which continues to persist alongside and blatantly ignores the stipulated legal age at marriage for girls, in total disregard of the educational laws of the land which make school attendance compulsory at basic level, not to mention the health and other socioeconomic consequences of such marriages on the life of the girl child.

We need also to consider the skewed socialisation process and gender role prescriptions which put unique demands on the labour of the *girl-child* such that she has to be the one whose right to education is sacrificed in order that she can be exploited to either assist in the upbringing of younger siblings or help in raising family income.

Women's internalised gender roles which cause them to put their own *health* needs last and rather focus on the health needs of their families are accountable for their unquestioning acceptance of unfair workloads which plague them with poor health. This is made worse by high fertility rates which result in high pregnancy-related mortality rates. The socialisation process and power relations which compel a woman to try to satisfy the child sex preferences of her husband through repeated childbirth and has been found to be dangerous for her health are the same factors which pressurise infertile women to strive fruitlessly to become fertile, sometimes at a cost to their lives. A related chauvinistic issue is the popularly entrenched assumption that childlessness of a couple is always attributable to the women.

Several governments have responded to the Declaration on the Elimination of Discrimination Against Women by enacting legislation to protect women who are victims of *violence.* Yet violence persists because it derives essentially from the lower status accorded to women in the family and society. Social inequality between the sexes is one contributory factor to women's subordinate position within the family. As a result, the disciplining of wives through battery is condoned by the structures which are expected to uphold the tenets of such laws, to the extent that sometimes fatal consequences of some cases of domestic violence are deliberately overlooked. When a judge in a homicide case tells a man that he was right in disciplining his wife for denying him sex but that he should have used an appropriate weapon, thereby trivialising the wife's death, then one can understand why this is a severe problem. When even a judge is convinced that a woman deserves to be beaten and even killed for asserting her right to her body, then who is the law intended to protect? While this case did not happen in Ghana similar actions by husbands are known.

The population policy which recognises the rights of couples and individuals to contraception is negated by marriage law provision which indirectly denies women their right to use periodic abstinence as a contraceptive method, by not recognising rape in marriage. The additional fact that most women enjoy their rights to contraception only at the pleasure of their spouses means that attempts to improve women's reproductive health rights could remain a difficult task in spite of all the other positive actions put in place and taken. The implied notion that a wife is the property of her husband is obviously at play in such circumstances.

The law against rape becomes a joke when female rape victims get blamed, interrogated and ridiculed as if they caused themselves to be raped, while the assailants are made to feel like heroes.

Female genital mutilation and other *harmful traditional practices* such as widowhood rites are prohibited by law, yet if society continues to manipulate women's minds and indirectly pressurise them into believing that their recognition and acceptance in society, as 'proper women', is linked to their adherence to such practices, then one can understand why the laws put in place will not protect them.

In trying to open up access to *political participation*, it is important to examine the psychological, social and cultural factors existing in society which either enable or disable the would-be female politician to accept her new or intended step as valid and acceptable, as well as prepare the people in her environment whose acceptance of the woman will give her the necessary support required to enable her actualise her hopes. It is obvious that female representation would provide the critical mass of gender balance needed to influence decision-making bodies, by integrating the views, needs and concerns of women. In order to prevent quotas from being used as token percentages that segregate women into marginal positions, it is important to ensure that the environment within which such women find themselves is positive, in terms of receptivity and nurturing. This alerts us to the need to examine the prevailing socialisation which instills and reinforces attitudes that stifle women's aspirations, as well as gender stereotyping jobs which dictate that politics is not a woman's turf.

The growing presence of women in the global *workforce* and in almost every field of business and enterprise is one of the great demographic trends of the century. However, as in politics, positions in top management and decision-making have often eluded women. Inequality in the public arena often reflects the pervasive inequality in the household. With male and female roles firmly entrenched in our society, women find it difficult to be taken seriously and step out of their traditional roles. When they do rise to the top, their potential is often underutilised. Stereotypes and misconceptions prevent organisations from appreciating their unique approaches to management and decision-making. Female managers are generally shut out of the 'old boys networks' and thus miss out on important information and opportunities for advancement on the job. Action is definitely needed to remove the 'glass ceilings' that thwart women's mobility. It is obvious that merely trying to close gaps through Affirmative Action and other measures do not always translate into improvements in women's situation.

As women work to change their long established status, to play a more active role in managing affairs of the nation, a concomitant change process is necessitated in men's situation. To bring about real improvements in the quality of women's lives, men must change also. We should not continue to over-exploit them with additional responsibilities to their families. Men need to be liberated in their thinking, attitudes and willingness to take a fairer share of the responsibilities and workloads which women now carry alone.

Conclusion

This chapter has tried to present some of the areas in which psycho-socio-cultural factors which may hinder the successful implementation of the Global Platform for Action which the world's women have struggled to produce. The need for change in the underlying beliefs and prejudices that do so much harm to women have been stressed. The role of men in implementation of the Platform for Action is an important issue which should not be underestimated. This can be difficult, since most of the changes that are required, will be threatening to men, whose dominant position may need to be modified. Obviously, well focused strategies will be needed, and should begin with women's own conscientisation, and subsequent redefinition of themselves for society. It will not be an easy task but with a determined leadership and the right partnership with men, success can and will be achieved.

As women work to change their long established subdued status, to play a more active role in managing affairs of the world, a concomitant change process is necessitated in men's situation, which may not be agreeable to them. Change will therefore require tact and involve a focused attempt to effect such actions with men themselves as partners. Men too need to be liberated in their thinking, attitudes and willingness to take a fairer share of the responsibilities and workloads that women now carry alone.

The effective promotion of gender equality requires that changes be effected in the values, behaviours and procedures within institutions whose work is to facilitate the implementation of the Platform for Action.

It is time to empower women everywhere to realise their potential to improve their quality of life and thus to build a better world for all. It is time to critically examine the context of the Ghanaian society bearing in mind the realities of sociocultural and structural impediments which constrain their progress.

Women need to:

- Begin to view personal achievements outside the home as worthwhile by de-emphasising reproductive roles as sole purposes in life.
- Determine how to deal with cultural and traditional expectations which cajole them into submission to oppression.
- Question negative images of women and redefine themselves from their own points of view.
- Decide on mechanisms to get and sustain their own representativeness into parliament or use their votes to create political constituencies and demand legitimacy and accountability of the political systems.
- Learn to be supportive of each other by purposely putting supportive mechanisms in place.
- Develop special awareness-raising and training efforts to positively enhance women's access to productive resources and determine how to prevent technology from displacing women from their traditional trades and replacing them with men.
- Ensure that the government commits itself to ensuring that International Conventions become national laws.
- Lobby for shifts in national spending priorities so as to reap tangible returns by ensuring resource reallocation to favour the social sector requirements.
- Evolve new strategies that give them autonomy over their bodies, satisfy their reproductive health needs and protect their physical, emotional and mental health.
- Ensure that girl-friendly mechanisms and incentives are put in place to make education more attractive to girls and parents, cause those who have already dropped out of school to re-enter the mainstream, and assure innovations for enhancing the entry of girls into scientific and technological fields of study.

This is the time to evolve new strategies that encourage international donors to provide advocacy alongside resource allocation. The international community needs to take actions that encourage the government to translate the Beijing Delegation's Commitment Statement into positive actions. Support is needed to develop institutional capacities in the area of gender mainstreaming to facilitate the integration of gender issues in normal governmental and non-governmental development sector work.

It is time for women to take action to persuade international agencies to specify what they will do differently. They need to be prevailed upon to not just provide funds but to make these funds responsive to the declared needs of women, so as to enable them to emerge from the bottom, to contribute more effectively in mainstream socioeconomic development.

4 Getting the Beijing Message into the Field

DR (MRS) NANA KONADU AGYEMAN RAWLINGS
FIRST LADY OF GHANA AND PRESIDENT OF THE 31ST
DECEMBER WOMEN'S MOVEMENT

The Significance of Beijing

The Beijing Declaration and Platform for Action, adopted unanimously at the World Conference on Women, does indeed reflect a new international commitment to the goals of equality, development and peace for all women everywhere. The Platform identified 12 'critical areas of concern'.

The success of the Platform for Action, an agenda for women's empowerment, will require a strong commitment on the part of the governments, international organisations and institutions at all levels. It will also require adequate mobilisation of resources at all levels as well as new and additional resources for the developing countries.

The Activities of the 31st December Women's Movement

The 31st December Women's Movement (DWM) is a development NGO, with a large membership involving women from all walks of life, but with the majority of its members being poor rural and urban women. The DWM in conjunction with the United Nations Development Programme (UNDP) organised a major workshop, which was financed by the Japanese Government, for women entrepreneurs in May, 1997.

The Movement has highlighted training as a crucial factor in the empowerment process. We have arranged skills-improvement training programmes using both formal and non-formal approaches. We have organised workshops and lectures using local languages for the benefit of those who had not had formal education and cannot speak English.

With the formal approach we have encouraged and insisted on education for girls throughout the educational structure. In the case of the informal approach, the training of women has been at the community level where they have been taken through the rudiments of book keeping, basic accounting methods, project management, capacity building etc.

Next, we dwelt on 'access to credit and capital' as a major obstacle for women's entrepreneurial development. We arranged to give small credit (between cedis 20,000–cedis 30,000 depending on the type of activity) to about 10,000 women initially – 1,000 women per region. We now have about 350,000 women benefiting from the scheme.

So far our women have proven to be very creditworthy. The repayment rate has been about 98 per cent and in some cases 100 per cent. The success of the small credit experiment has encouraged us to establish a Credit and Loans Saving Scheme (CLSS) for women in the low income bracket who are willing, and are able, to embark on income-generation projects.

Our Credit and Loans Saving Scheme attracts a very low interest rate, certainly lower than the lending rates of the formal Banks, and has flexible payment terms. The scheme exhibits very little or no bureaucracy, compared to that of formal banks, all aimed at minimising the frustration that our poor women suffer when they attempt to get into an income-generation project. The DWM has been involved in the setting up of a Revolving Credit Facility for individual or groups of women engaged in economic activity.

We have introduced and encouraged transfer of appropriate technology to ensure competence, efficiency and capability of our women in cottage industry, agriculture, micro-enterprise, etc.

Political empowerment has been a critical factor in all our efforts. It is our belief that women, constituting 50 per cent of the population should not be completely left out of the policy and decision-making process. Accordingly we have, relentlessly, advocated for the consideration, and appointment of capable women to high office or executive positions both in the public and private sectors of the economy. We have also encouraged women to contest for political office at district, regional and national levels.

However, looking at the 1996 general election results we realise that we need to intensify our efforts at involving women in political decision-making.

On the important issue of reproductive rights and health, the DWM has been very active in family planning and population education programmes using the medium of community theatre. We have procured mobile cinema vans to assist in this exercise. We are constantly reminding our rural folk and the general population on the direct relation of population to the development of the family unit, as well as the nation as a whole.

Conclusion: Maintaining the Momentum of Beijing

The DWM is still very active, pursuing programmes geared towards the realisation of the objectives of the Beijing Platform for Action. We believe that the practical approach we have adopted will, without doubt, make a positive impact on the lives of the women as well as other vulnerable groups in our society.

5   Gender Goals of the Immediate Past

DR MARY GRANT[1]
CHAIRPERSON OF THE NATIONAL COUNCIL FOR WOMEN AND
DEVELOPMENT, GHANA

The Product of Past International Attention

The first three world conferences on women focused on the need for the global emancipation of women and provided the international community and national governments with the necessary blueprint towards that end. Important success stories have been registered in many countries. The fact however remains that worldwide, today, there are many poor and disadvantaged women, more unemployed women and greater insecurity among women than there was 10 years ago.

Even though many meetings have been held to address various aspects of the problem, women are today still faced with major obstacles in translating their goals into reality. The majority of women worldwide continue to occupy lower positions on the employment ladder, women are battered in homes and continue to constitute the silent victims of wars. Women's rights are violated. Women and children continue to suffer in Africa during times of war. In times of war when the peace is disturbed, development paths charted by women in their struggle for emancipation are reversed. We also recognise that there is still much to be done for our women especially the urban poor, rural women, the girl child,[2] the aged and women with disability.

The Need to Add New Gender Goals

Our task as women leaders is therefore to change this trend and I personally hold the view that without the active participation of women and the incorporation of gender perspectives at all levels of decision-making, our ultimate goals of equality, development and peace cannot be attained.

To address the above problems, I would propose that as a matter of urgency in the coming decade, new priority areas like the issue of armed conflict, displaced persons, refugees and violence against women be given serious consideration.

The international community needs to show commitment by providing the necessary financial and other resources to help make the process of economic recovery felt by the people.

Attention should be given to formal education with the emphasis on the girl child. Attention should also be given to issues on women's reproductive health and rights, the environment as well as women's access to economic and productive resources.

The status of National Machineries and relevant women-centred NGOs should be strengthened to enable them to effectively address the challenges and demands of women worldwide.

Greater intensification of political education should be made to urge more women to participate in political activities and to stand for and be voted into political offices.

Women should play an active role in peace initiatives, conflict prevention, management and resolution both at the national and international levels. Women all over the world must come together and work to achieve peace.

World leaders are to be called to acknowledge the fact that our goals of equality, development and peace require continuous effort to prevent and eliminate wars and other major sources of social distress and instability within societies globally. Women should tell the war mongers the world over that the world is tired of wars.

Democracy should be practised at all levels both in the homes and communities. Then it will have a chance to work nationally and internationally.

Last but not the least women should continue to speak with one voice as women and thus for all mankind.

Notes

1   Editors' note: Dr Mary Grant was a member of the Council of State of the Republic of Ghana. As Chairperson of the National Council for Women and Development, she was an active advocate of gender equality in Ghana, attended Beijing and publicised the Beijing message through the media, most importantly in a society where there are high levels of female illiteracy through television.

2   The 'girl child' was a special feature of the African Platform for Action at Beijing – African women brought this focus realising that the socialisation of the girl child is mother to the experience of women.

6 An Overview of Ghanaian Gender Activity

DR NAANA AGYEMANG-MENSAH
GENDER SPECIALIST, ASSID, GHANA AND
PROFESSOR NANA ARABA APT,
DIRECTOR OF THE CENTRE FOR SOCIAL POLICY STUDIES,
GHANA

Introduction

This chapter discusses the various strategies applied by different institutions and organisations in continued attempts to reduce gender disparities in Ghana. The effectiveness of the strategies are discussed in light of the impact on women's lives using information from national surveys and census data.

Ghana like other countries started to address women's marginalisation by focusing on women's welfare and reproductive needs. Community development approaches were used to address the basic needs of communities, and women were assisted with skills, services and resources to enable them to perform their reproductive roles better.

Attention to gender issues gained momentum after the 1975 World Conference on Women which highlighted the need to integrate women into development. A national machinery, the National Council for Women and Development (NCWD), was set up in 1975 as the mouth piece of women and the agency responsible for ensuring women's integration into development. Between 1976 and 1978, a series of studies commissioned by the NCWD highlighted gender inequalities and discriminations in women's access to resources, services and facilities which were critical to their development. The most disturbing revelations included the severity of poverty among the female population, discriminatory cultural and traditional practices and the unusually high rates of female illiteracy. The NCWD's desire to mount a literacy campaign at the time was not immediately acceptable to women, who overwhelmingly demanded assistance with economic self-sufficiency. This was understandable since the women needed to reduce their poverty, and develop a degree of economic empowerment that would enable them to take actions to improve their general welfare and thus facilitate their enhanced contribution to national development.

Later, it became necessary to shift emphasis to women's productive roles as against the previous focus in development projects on their reproductive roles. Subsequently the emphasis moved from welfare and family oriented programmes to economic and social resources development as tools to rectify gender differentials.

Gender activities in Ghana have therefore utilised a multiplicity of strategies including

* economic empowerment through entrepreneurship development,
* traditional technology improvement,
* advocacy and lobbying,
* capacity building,
* policy reforms and legislation,
* education and training,
* literacy education,
* extension services,
* mobilisation.

These efforts have been targeted predominantly at poor rural women who have been identified as the most needy of assistance. This has to some extent been done to the disadvantage of equally poor women in urban areas who have often been obscured by the apparent affluence around them.

Gender activities directed at the more enlightened in the female population have focused on improving their decision-making participation at policy-making levels on gender sensitisation, political education, advocacy, and the lobbying of government for affirmative action, particularly in the appointment of qualified people to policy-making bodies.

Economic Empowerment

Business development as a strategy for reducing gender inequalities appears to have been the single most common strategy in Ghana. It has in fact been used as an entry point for projects in family planning, health and literacy programmes in recent times. Women's generally poor economic status has caused the majority of the interventions by both the NCWD and other agencies to focus on economic emancipation. While this method was initially pursued with the objective of promoting equality and enhancing efficiency in production, the strategy became even more important during the Structural Adjustment Era when cuts in social spending increased women's need to generate more resources to secure access to basic services such as health care, as well as enhance contribution to community development projects.

Women are assisted by providing them with access to economic resources, to services and to skills training. Specific activities have included

- the provision of improved technologies to enhance productivity and reduce labour inputs,
- improving access to credit facilities,
- vocational skills training,
- nutrition education and health education,
- the provision of farm support services to small holder farmers (in groups) to enhance food production, processing, storage and transportation to markets.

Appropriate Technology and Labour Saving Devices

With the promotion of income-generating activities it became necessary to ensure efficient, lucrative and manageable production through the introduction of appropriate technologies to upgrade the traditional methods and sometimes change production methods.

Social and productive technologies have been developed with the former saving labour and time, and the latter increasing production, and sometimes saving time as well. Broad looms for weaving have been introduced and accepted in areas where weaving used to be taboo for women and new types of looms have opened up avenues for income earning.

While many of the technologies have saved time and labour and even increased production, some have at the same time led to a reduction in the degree of control women have been able to wield over their projects, especially where the mode of operation of the technology has necessitated the involvement of men as partners or hired labour. There have been cases where some men have used their involvement as machine operators or owners to determine when and what quantity of raw materials a women or group may process at a time (Agyemang-Mensah, 1988). Such loss of control tends to affect not only the autonomy of the women but also their productivity levels. It is important therefore to make technology 'operable and maintainable' by women themselves.

The overuse of women's scarce time and energies on projects which sometimes tend to yield them few positive results has been noted in some cases. This has not been made known to those who need to know because impact analysis of economic projects has been virtually nil. Many projects have been evaluated by external consultants who have often keyed in on project implementation and the use of budgeted resources as against using pre- and post project evaluation to judge the values gained by project beneficiaries.

Many income-generating projects have not given much attention to measures to guarantee markets for the products. The result is that farmers, especially those using irrigation, incur losses, due to gluts at harvest times. Currently an average of 40 per cent of crops perish (FAO, n.d.). Poor infrastructure such as feeder roads and transportation have affected women's ability to cart food crops from the farms. Women have been found to carry up to two head loads of 30kg over an average of 5km a day (World Bank, 1991). This means a lot of back breaking efforts with little benefits for many women. Apart from this, little attempt is made to ensure that market information gets to them or that prices of items are such that they are able to make profits.

The needs of women who prefer to work individually instead of in groups have not been addressed. This can be done through the establishment of community resource centres at which trained personnel either from the local area or otherwise can be stationed to provide timely technical assistance.

Improvements are required in the kinds of innovations introduced for home use, since many of women's daily chores involve a lot of strain and time wastage. Simple transportation technologies are necessary to reduce the amount of walking that women do. Their outmoded tools for farming which are a source of great discomfort and ill health also require upgrading.

Facilitation of Access to Credit

After initiating income-generating projects, women's need for credit and other resources became glaring. Initial efforts were mustered by the NCWD through its advocacy role to obtain grants and other technical assistance from foreign donors and land from traditional leaders. The reluctance of local banks to give loans to women caused the NCWD to lend support to the establishment of the Ghana branch of the Women's World Banking whose main body had had two prominent Ghanaian women as founding members. Since 1983, the bank has used its role as a guarantee bank to secure funds from local credit institutions for subsequent disbursement to women's groups. Mostly the credit has gone for fixed assets, as working capital, for the construction of project sites, etc. Within the past two decades, several schemes have been evolved to provide credit for women, without strict adherence to procedures followed by formal credit institutions. Other women fund themselves through their group member' contributions and dues.

A significant feature of most of these schemes in the combination of credit with management skills training and other conditions which ensure repayment of loans by recipients. The effectiveness of peer pressure is remarkable and accounts for the high rates of repayment. Experience from the ENOWID projects (these were implemented to buffer the harsh effects of structural adjustment policies on women) showed that repayment could be as high as 97 per cent and 100 per cent in a few cases (NCWD Project Files). Business educators who were put in place to oversee payments helped to ensure sustainability of the scheme and acted as a buffer against default in repayment of loans.

In the case of the Women's World Banking, women are mobilised into groups and trained in business management and record keeping skills before loans are granted. Regular monitoring of projects has also been an important feature.

Effective as these schemes have been in many cases, it is noteworthy that only moderate impact has been made in terms of the numbers which require assistance. In a recent study, only 10–20 per cent of women interviewed had the required set of pots, calabashes and simple tools that they required for their small businesses. In another study, as much as 92 per cent of respondents indicated that they were unable to purchase raw materials and store them in the peak session for later use, due to their lack of access to credit (FAO, n.d.). It is necessary therefore to assess the effectiveness of the several schemes so that the best ones are developed and expanded to cover more women.

Rural banks have spread around the country except for the three northern regions where only four currently exist (Bortei Doku, 1991). However while these banks do give loans to women, figures from a rural bank on the proportion of credit given between 1984–88 by gender indicates that the amounts of loans for men increased from 77 per cent to 88 per cent in 1988 while that for women declined from 23 per cent in 1984 to 12 per cent in 1988. It was also noted that loans to cocoa farmers (mostly men) increased from 25 per cent in 1984 to 85 per cent in 1988, while loans for food crop farmers (mostly women) declined from 57 per cent in 1984 to five per cent in 1988 (Opoku, 1989). Many rural enterprises are unable to take advantage of these banks because of the distance from home to the banks and the waiting periods involved. They therefore resort to the use of local sources such as money lenders and supplier's credit which affect profits considerably.

Land Acquisition

Facilitating marketing as a strategy received very little attention in earlier projects in spite of the awareness that many women not only lacked market information, but did not have the freedom to travel away from home easily. Fortunately, in the few instances where attempts have been made to hire out trucks to individuals and groups to cart food crops to market centres fruitful results have been noticeable and the funds generated have gone into revolving loan funds.

According to FAO, the high cost of transportation and the poor state of roads is the single most important factor affecting the ability of subsistence farmers to enter the market economy. It goes on to say that the average rural woman walks 1,000 hours per annum (FAO, ndp). Obviously the need to ameliorate this situation through assistance with transportation, storage and outlets for marketing goods cannot be understated.

Attempts have also been made by some donors to provide silos for grains drying and storage without much success since some women tend to prefer their individual storage facilities to communal storage in silos. The implication is that beneficiaries should be consulted on projects expected to benefit them.

Integrated Projects

The low impact of projects which focused on single areas such as health, family planning or income-generation in the early 1980s has given way to more integrated approaches. Time has shown that single projects are not only time wasting but ineffective in fulfilling women's many needs. It has become necessary for project designers to consider women's multiple roles in the development of project objectives so as to provide them with useful skills that enable them to perform their many roles effectively.

Advocacy

The NCWD has used advocacy as an effective strategy in trying to promote gender equality in Ghana. As the official liaison body between women's groups and government, its chief task has been to ensure that the government hears the 'concerns' of women. It has accordingly submitted a total of 10 Memoranda and Recommendations to Government since 1975, on a number of issues affecting women, with the latest being a submission on Affirmative Action, which was submitted after the Beijing Conference. Through its efforts the Law Reform Commission was established in 1975 to examine certain laws which negatively affected women's welfare and in 1985 succeeded in getting the government to enact four laws which sought to safeguard the access of women, particularly those married under the Customary Law, to their inherited property.

In 1987 the NCWD lobbied the Ghana government to ratify the United Nations Convention on the Elimination of all forms of Discrimination Against Women (CEDAW) and has submitted two reports so far to the CEDAW Committee on the 'Situation of women in Ghana'. As part of the NCWD's post-Beijing actions, the CEDAW Monitoring Committee has been set up and a study commissioned to examine how the CEDAW provisions can be effectively integrated into the laws of the land.

In 1991 the NCWD with other women's groups sent a memorandum to the Consultative Assembly which was drafting the present Constitution, requesting that certain provisions, which sought to change selected sociocultural practices inimical to women, be included in the draft document. These included measures aimed at eradicating female genital mutilation and widowhood rites. Laws on these have since been passed.

Apart from the NCWD, several NGOs initiated by women are using advocacy to address gender inequalities. The Ghana Association for Women's Welfare (GAWW) has through advocacy, lobbied traditional rulers in parts of the Northern and Upper regions where female genital mutilation and other harmful traditional practices are carried out to enact bye-laws prohibiting such practices.

Gender Awareness Creation

Realising that the lack of success with development projects could be traced to loopholes in the planning and implementation process, specifically to planners' lack of awareness and consideration of gender issues, the NCWD organised a series of Gender Awareness Regional workshops for sector policy-makers and development practitioners in 1990.

The assumption was that some of the basic interests of women at the family and community levels were being inadvertently overlooked by these power actors and thus causing them to adopt strategies that did not highlight and cater to the unique situation and needs of women. Unfortunately however in most cases, the top policy-makers themselves did not attend the workshops but sent junior officers who often had no authority in decision-making.

The NCWD by virtue of its position as the national machinery for women's advancement serves on several sector and inter-sector planning committees and utilises the opportunity to focus their discussion on gender issues. It has also organised several workshops on topical issues, aimed at drawing attention to women's situation in general.

Associates in Development (ASSID), an NGO has initiated a Gender Awareness programme targeted at secondary school girls in an attempt to sensitise them early to the existing inequalities in order to motivate them to want to strive to make a difference in women's marginalised position in society.

Government Policy and Legislative Measures

It is noteworthy that successive governments have initiated several positive measures without prompting.

The institution of rural banks has served to open hitherto closed doors to women in the rural areas especially, even though the extent of their benefits is not comparable to that of rural men.

The primary health care policy was intended to facilitate easy access of rural people, the majority of whom are women to health care and to promote their participation in health care provision. The present involvement of TBAs (traditional birth attendants) as trained first aid providers is significant.

The new pension scheme and the expansion of the social security scheme to cover informal sector employees are all measures to include women who form the bulk of informal sector workers who are mostly self employed. How they take advantage of these schemes is however another matter. The need for education, information and confidence building cannot be underrated.

The decentralisation policy was clearly intended to increase the participation of rural folks including women in decision-making at the local level. The selection process prescribed by the government for the Consultative Assembly membership which allocated specified spaces for the NCWD and the women's organisations turned out to be virtually the only avenues which permitted women entry into the constitution drafting group, 25 out of the 258 members were female. This process set the stage for women's participation in the recent presidential and parliamentary elections. Most of the constitution drafters developed enough confidence to stand for parliamentary and District Assembly elections.

Unfortunately in the present District Assemblies, women form only 6.6 per cent of the membership and many of them were appointed.

The numbers are not only illustrative of the sociocultural context but also the kind of women forming the percentages requires scrutiny. The need for conscientisation and empowerment of the ordinary women is an issue needing serious attention.

Capacity Building

To make for sustainability and to ensure that skills reach down to grassroots women, the training of para-professionals has become a useful strategy to disseminate information. Women's group leaders are increasingly being trained in a variety of areas, to go and train or inform others in their groups and communities. In water and sanitation projects, women have been trained as Community Water Organisers (CWOs) to impart health information to women in their communities, as well as take care of hand pump maintenance.

Non-formal Education

It is a fact in Ghana that formal education has bypassed women. In 1990 the illiteracy rates for women were 49 per cent compared to 30 per cent for men. In extreme cases, such as in parts of Northern Ghana about 70 per cent of women have never been to school. The non-formal education programme has therefore been identified as a useful strategy that attempts to fill the knowledge gap created by the lack of access to formal education. It is no doubt indicative therefore that 54 per cent of the programme's learners were women (NCWD, 1994).

The Non-formal Education (NFED) Programme has diversified from the common curriculum of reading and writing with some attention to home management and income-generating skills acquisition, to include a much wider spectrum of themes in family life education, population education, legal literacy, etc. Workshops, seminars and lectures of all kinds have been undertaken and the media networks have been utilised to disseminate information.

Literacy Education

Literacy education has been undertaken by several projects as important components. Currently almost all NGO and sector ministries operating projects with women have undertaken literacy education with the contents carefully chosen to relate to women's daily needs in health, agriculture, home life, economic enterprises, etc.

Unfortunately however even though women form 63 per cent (ROG/ UNICEF, 1990) of the total learning population, the number of female teachers has not been large enough to ensure motivation for enrolment and retention. Another issue is that of utility. Even though learners have reading materials, the fact that learners are still very illiterate as far as interaction in official circles is concerned is an issue for concern since they remain marginalised as far as communication in English, the official language, is concerned. While the NFED officials intend to equip the learners first with literacy skills in their own languages before proceeding to the official language – English – one wonders if adult women who tend to have very little time have to be put through this long process in view of their ages and other responsibilities.

Leadership and Management Training

Women's projects in the early 1980s tended to stress access to technology and then credit, without much attention to capacity building. With the failure of many groups to stay together due to poor leadership and improper financial accounting, efforts at skills training begun. Currently, almost all women's projects in income-generation include training in bookkeeping, leadership skills, management and simple accounting as important components.

Vocational Training

Vocational skills acquisition forms a major category in non-formal education activities. Both private as well as government institutions are involved in providing skills, particularly to young women.

Unfortunately however it has been noted that not many women are able to take advantage of such facilities because of the few spaces available for 'women's courses' in the few government institutions. What is more the timing of classes disable many young people who also have to earn an income during the day from participating. More seriously, the curriculum designated for women tends to be very limiting and does not enable them to develop the courage to enter 'non-traditional' fields. The lapse in educational planning requires reorientation. Though other private institutions exist for girls, these are also restricted to tuition in the traditional fields of dressmaking, home management, hairdressing and cookery, are quite expensive. The unfortunate fact again is that even though many women enter cookery, few get into higher paying positions as chefs of hotels and restaurants. These positions get taken up by the few males who enter the profession.

Women Empowering Women

Several women's organisations have realised their responsibility to their less fortunate sisters and have taken steps to assist them through capacity building projects.

The 31st December Women's Movement has excelled in income-generation and the provision of day care centres to allow women to work without disturbances.

FIDA has exemplified excellent gender practice in promoting legal reforms, providing legal aid services and creating legal awareness through a number of public fora. Within the past year, the Associates in Development (ASSID) which aims at creating a pool of grassroots para-legal professionals to assist rural women in deprived areas of Upper West Region, has added its weight to the legal education efforts, using an innovative three tier training of trainers process to train both literate and illiterate grassroots women to educate their own families, socioeconomic groups and communities in the laws affecting women and children. Through this process, hard-to-reach women are given access to legal information and assistance by people they know and trust.

The Ghana Registered Midwives Association (GRMA) in conjunction with the Ministry of Health has trained several traditional birth attendants (TBAs) to not only take care of child deliveries but also to take care of the minor health needs of rural women and their children. Some TBAs currently provide first aid, family planning services (non-prescriptive) mobilise for immunisation and educate their communities on personal and environmental hygiene. This is a big relief since only 45 per cent of rural people have access to health care (ROG/UNICEF, 1990) and majority of rural people are women, 65 per cent of whose deliveries are handled by untrained persons (MCH/FP, Annual Report 1992). A National TBA Training Programme Secretariat was established in 1994 to provide multiple health services to isolated rural women who would otherwise forego health services. The GRMA has performed with distinction alongside the Ministry of Health in its attempt at reducing maternal mortality rates through family planning service provision and safe motherhood initiatives.

The Women in Science and Technology (WIST) group in a bid to steer girls away from traditional courses seen as women's fields, into science and technological fields, has in conjunction with the Ministry of Education instituted annual science clinics to motivate senior secondary school girls studying science and mathematics to remain in their chosen fields.

Mobilisation

A study of women's activities in 1976 led to the realisation that women's individual economic activities were not enabling them to gain access to useful resources. Since then, the NCWD and other groups have mobilised women into groups along occupational lines in order to gain them access to credit, land, grants, machinery, educational programmes, etc.

In agriculture, group formation has been useful in enabling women to receive technical information from male extension workers with whom they previously could not interact due to cultural inhibitions, in areas where women are debarred from interacting with males who are not family members.

Mobilisation of women at the grassroots level has been an effective tool utilised by the 31st December Women's Movement (DWM) which has been a trail blazer in political awareness creation and action, particularly the exercise of their right to vote. Their use of slogans and songs has been particularly effective.

Extension

In the absence of large stocks of human and material resources, it has been very important to utilise extension strategies in taking development activities to widely dispersed people, especially those in rural areas. The Ministries of

Health and Agriculture have particularly utilised extension methods for women's benefit although a lot still remains to be done to improve women farmers' access to information and skills in the use of productive technology.

This is because in agriculture the extension curriculum for women has about 40 per cent of the time devoted to nutrition and home management issues with the rest of the time being for farming improvement. In view of the fact that contact time is very limited, the effect of agricultural extension on women's activities has been less than desirable. For instance the Ashanti region with the highest number of 308,547 female farmers in 1984 had only 1.1 per cent coverage in 1987 while Greater Accra with 26,074 women had 17.9 per cent coverage (World Bank, 1991). To increase effectiveness, it may be necessary for agricultural extension workers to focus on farming improvement and post-harvest issues so that the Nutrition Division of the Ministry of Health or Non-Formal Education Division (NFED) takes over the other aspects of their present curriculum.

In agriculture, as well as in health, the important roles which women play as producers, reproducers and nurturers, are imperatives for serious actions.

Beneficiary Participation

While there has been a shift from the welfare approach of giving things to rural people to getting them to participate in projects, a cursory look at strategies indicate that their participation has not been effective. Their participation continues to be limited to contribution of resources such as labour, land, stones and sand for construction of a shed for instance, or to contribution of matching funds, and not to the planning process (Agyemang-Mensah, 1988).

Many of women's projects are planned from the outside and taken to them. Sometimes a project is even written by expatriate consultants who hardly know anything about the areas where implementation is to take place. Evaluation is almost always done by external consultants. The fact of women's ability to determine effective programmes for themselves elude many project staff. It is not surprising therefore that women have been at times criticised for being apathetic and ignorant when they really were just not interested and wished rather to spend their time on other more viable ventures.

Obviously beneficiary participation cannot remain a wish. It should be nurtured through capacity building which facilitates effective involvement of beneficiaries in the evolution as well as the implementation and impact assessment of given projects.

Conclusion: Towards a Strategy for a Beneficial Integration of Women into Development

In this chapter, we have identified the existing potential economic inputs of women, reviewed gender strategies and activities in order to highlight their weaknesses and strengths, obstacles and barriers should therefore be used as a step towards planning for a better recognition and compensation of women for their economic and social role in nation building. This entails a lifelong planning for women from birth to old age. Policies and programmes need to take into consideration the implications of existing trends. Preventive measures are equally necessary for while curative measures may ease conditions, only preventive measures can avoid women entering the state of inequality and vulnerability in the future.

In this respect it is necessary to invest in the girl child in order to avoid future vulnerability. Education, training, health and employment are preventive actions that should take prominence as starting capital for the women of the future. A life course approach to development planning in respect of women to include a targeted approach for each age cohort of females is more than necessary. Technical assistance in aid of women should therefore take cognisance of the factor of lifetime planning to be able to give young and middle age women the necessary take off for their older years.

To begin with an area that so far women's organisations have been silent on is the empowerment of older women. On the government side, problems engendered by the customary rules of succession and widowhood in Ghana have received serious attention. In line with United Nations plan of action on the need to protect vulnerable groups within the ageing populations, Ghana has taken special measures with regard to older women who are in the main widows (Apt, 1994, pp. 53–63).

There is a need for the recognition of older women's role in human capital. In Ghana it is substantial (Apt van Ham, 1993; Apt, 1996) and important especially in the agricultural sector. They produce and make agricultural commodities but of most importance, they are food producers, processors and marketers. Older women nevertheless need incentives. Through training, provision of extension services and credit facilities, older women can be assisted in carrying out their productive work in a more efficient and beneficial manner.

The well-being of older women in Ghana is directly related to their social and environmental circumstances and their ability to cope with those circumstances. They face hardships which are directly linked to their economic conditions. The main reason for the economic hardship is partly cultural and partly due to the fact that existing pensions and social security schemes cover a very small proportion of the female population. With the decreasing of family support linked to migration patterns in the country, the vulnerability of older women should become important matters for technical assistance programmes.

On the whole, women continue to occupy the lower levels of the social and economic and political ladder. Still fewer girls than boys enter school and more girls than boys drop out of school before they can reap the benefits of schooling. More sick boys receive medical attention than girls and child mortality rates for girls is 10 per cent higher than that for boys.

Maternal mortality has not improved substantially and women's health continues to receive attention mainly when they are pregnant or lactating. Women's nutrition levels have not improved in spite of all the economic activities and about 60 per cent of pregnant women are anaemic. Women with information about family planning methods and service outlets still do not use contraceptives even when they do not wish to have more children because their spouses who wield control over their bodies do not agree to family planning.

Female farm holders are only 33 per cent when women form 52 per cent of the bulk of agricultural workers and produce the bulk of the nation's subsistence crops.

It is evident from the above that a reorientation of approaches is necessary to identify the root causes of gender inequality and to redress the situation with those for whose benefit projects are planned. It is possible that maybe women's poverty has been misinterpreted as being due to underdevelopment, instead of viewing it as a result of their subordinate position. There have been instances where men have assumed control over women's projects or when women have been unable to repay loans because their husbands have beaten them into surrendering their loans for their own personal use. Women may not have needed more income-generation activities but rather changes in financial responsibilities between them and their spouse, in view of the fact that more income has meant increased financial responsibilities for women and fewer for men.

Indeed increases in women's economic participation in the informal sector where they abound has for some meant more dependence on the girl child's assistance in carrying out both household chores and economic activities. In many cases, women's activities have been wrongly increased while nothing has been done about the unfair gender division of labour which saps their energies and leaves them no time for rest or leisure. It is time to make deliberate efforts to ensure proper coordination of women's projects by donors, NGOs and governmental bodies. This will not only ensure proper use of resources, but will also preserve women's time and energies.

Women's access to credit may have been eased to some extent but not their access to the important factors of production, such as land, which many are debarred by tradition from owning. Besides, women's businesses have remained micro and small scale. Maybe it is time to ensure that some women's businesses grow into medium scale businesses which can be mainstreamed.

It is obvious that the impact of sociocultural constraints have been critical. This is why conscientisation of women to their status and position in society and the important roles they play is essential to their ability to respond to external inputs. Empowerment, which gives women control over themselves and their destinies is of great importance and implies in-depth social, economic and political shifts. Attention needs to be focused on effecting changes in existing social relations, gender division of labour and the attitudes held about women which foster denial and trivialisation of gender issues, and thus promote the tendency to attack symptoms rather than the underlying causes of women's unequal status.

Massive gender sensitisation programmes and capacity building for the mainstreaming of gender issues in national policies require attention. Disaggregated data which highlight existing gender inequalities and allow comparisons between women's and men's contributions to national development, and the constraints they face, which are specific to their gender, will be helpful in persuading policy-makers to evolve gender sensitive policies.

Advocacy to foster access not only to resources and credit but more importantly to decision-making power is necessary to effect the needed changes and women themselves should begin to believe that tradition and culture are dynamic and therefore mobilise for collective action to acknowledge, analyse and challenge prevailing institutionalised gender discrimination and inequalities. Partnership with men as advocates for women's equality with men is necessary if changes are to be effected in existing power relations.

References

Agyemang-Mensah, N. (1988), *An examination of the nature and extent of rural women's participation in income generating projects*, doctoral dissertation, Michigan State University.
Agyemang-Mensah, N. (1992), 'Employment opportunities in forestry for women', paper presented at the *Workshop on Women and Forestry*, organised by the ITTO and the 31st December Women's Movement.

Agyemang-Mensah, N. (1994), 'Review of strategies (adopted) for the advancement of women in rural development in Ghana (1975 to date)' in *Strategies for the sustained advancement of women in rural areas*, report of International Workshop, Accra, Ghana, 15–20 November 1993, pp. 53–65.

Apt van Ham, N.A. (1993), *Help for self-help: Elderly African women ahead of development*, The XIth International Congress on Gerontology, Budapest, Working Paper 4.

Apt van Ham, N.A. (1994), 'Ghana', *Legislation affecting older people in developed and developing countries*, EAGLE and IFA.

Apt, N.A. (1996), *Coping with old age in a changing Africa*, Avebury: Aldershot.

Bortei Doku, E. (1990), *A profile of women in Ghana*, prepared on behalf of the Canada High Commission.

Brown, C.K. (1976), 'Towards a meaningful approach to the organisaton of rural development in Ghana', *Journal of Sociology* ,Vol. 10, No. 1, pp. 32–42.

FAO (no date), *Development of a rural agro industries programme*, final report by FAO Mission.

Gaisie, S.K. and Degraft Johnson, K.T., (1974), *Population of Ghana*, CICRED Publication.

Ghana Statistical Service (1984), *Population Census of Ghana, 1984.*

Ghana Statistical Service (1989), *Ghana Demographic Health Survey*, (GDHS) final report.

Ghana Statistical Service (1989), *Ghana Living Standards Survey*, (GLSS) final report.

Ghana Statistical Service (1993), *Ghana Living Standards Survey*, (GLSS).

ILO (1990), *Women learn from each other: Report on South African and Namibia Women leaders study tour of successful women's productive and income generating projects in Ghana*, (Project NLM/89/MOI/NOR).

Ministry of Health, MCH/FP (1992), *Annual Report 1992.*

National Council on Women and Development (1984), *Annual Report 1980–84.*

National Council on Women and Development (1994), *Situation on women in Ghana (1985–1994)*, report to the 4th World Conference on Women.

Opoku, I. (1989), *Gender differences and access to credit: an example of the Kwahu Praso Area*, BA Long essay, University of Ghana, Legon, Ghana.

Republic of Ghana/UNICEF (1990), *Children and women of Ghana: a situation analysis, 1989–90*, Accra.

Twumasi, Kojo (1993), *Enhancing opportunities for women in development and evaluation of project implementation*, prepared for the Ministry of Local Government and Rural Development.

UNECA (1989), *Report to the Fourth Regional Conference on the Integration of Women in Development on the Implementation of the Arusha Strategies for Advancement of Women in Africa: regional perspective.*

World Bank (1991), *Ghana Medium Term Agricultural Development Strategy (MTADS): An agenda for sustained growth and development 1991–2000*, Vol. 1.

7 Enterprising Women: The Business of Building Women's Economic Networks – the Ghanaian Association of Women Entrepreneurs Contribution

LUCIA QUAKYE
GAWE, GHANA

Introduction

The inability of Africa's economy to turn the tide of underdevelopment – low food production levels, balance of payment difficulties, inflation, rapid population growth, low or negative GDP growth rates, declines in social services and standards, etc., have brought to the fore discussions on the role of women entrepreneurs and the development of the informal productive sector, if Africa is to make any headway. Lately, attention has begun to fall on the use and benefits of 'alternative approaches' to development. It is this new policy setting that brings about the need to explore the potential contribution of women entrepreneurs in the informal and small scale industrial sector to Africa's economic recovery and development.

Entrepreneurship in all its diversity in Africa provides a dynamic and potentially efficient means of meeting many of the emerging challenges of the development and debt crisis in Africa. Entrepreneurship in the African context remains concerned with the 'graduation' of informal sector ventures with a realistic business prospectus to better established and endowed enterprises, as well as with promoting economic diversification, export to niche market, future growth and higher living standards. African women entrepreneurs have a matured long standing tradition of entrepreneurship for centuries. In the context of ongoing reforms and rethinking of development: this puts women entrepreneurs in a pivotal position in relation to the expectation and expansion of economic development.

A number of United Nations Resolutions have stressed the importance of developing indigenous entrepreneurial capabilities as a means of accelerating recovery and sustaining development. The Arusha and Nairobi Forward-looking Strategies for the Advancement of Women as well as the Abuja Declaration of Participatory Development (which defined the role of women in Africa in the '90s), have also emphasized the importance of enhancing women entrepreneurship as a means of increasing their contribution to economic recovery and development.

These strategies urgently demand that concrete efforts be made to develop stronger links between women entrepreneurs at all levels to strengthen women's capabilities to deal and cope with the increasing challenges of the global market.

It is against this background, the GAWE initiated and organised the First Global Women Entrepreneurs Trade Fair and Investment Forum – the first of its kind.[1]

Statements and Views of Participants in the First Global Women Entrepreneurs Trade Fair and Investment Forum – 26 June–3 July, 1996, Accra

Dr K.Y. Amoaku, Executive Secretary of the UNECA (United Nations Economic Commission for Africa) in his statement at the above forum assured participants that the UNECA remains a constant ally in women's economic empowerment. In this regard, a Leadership Fund has been established by the UNECA to provide funding for entrepreneurial development programmes for women.

He mentioned that entrepreneurship in Africa remains the main vehicle of future growth, better living standards and increasing of self-reliance. Entrepreneurship is seen by most African policy-makers as significant and having an increasing role in the 1990s and beyond in reducing unemployment and income disparities between social groups in both rural and urban areas, and in alleviating the negative effects of structural adjustment measures.

He commended African women entrepreneurs for applying production technologies and processes to their markets and resource environment. However, they need to be assisted in order to grow and be able to take advantage of the national and regional market opportunities. A key element in this regard is for national policies to move towards opening boundaries between neighbouring states.

Dr Ada S. Adler, a representative of the United States from the Department of State for African Affairs in her statement in the same forum stressed that Africa's potential for economic growth rest on the dual foundation of democracy and free enterprise. These values go hand-in-hand and support one another because both democracy and free enterprise depend on predictability and the rule of law. The private sector is a more dynamic and innovative force for development than government and Africa must look more and more to the private sector to provide leadership in moving forward.

She emphasised that governments must not overlook the economic value of the informal sector and the small and medium-sized enterprises; many of which are run by women. Africa's decision-makers must therefore address specific needs of women and smaller firms and not only focus on large companies making large investments.

Dr Adler further emphasized that the task for African governments is to create an enabling environment by removing constraints to political and economic freedom and to encourage greater individual participation. A country with a transparent legal system under which an investor can be aware of all the relevant laws and regulations and be assured of their enforcement, encourages both domestic and foreign investment.

Strategies for Women Entrepreneurs to Effectively Compete in the Global Economy

The effectiveness of coming together of women entrepreneurs in Africa and the rest of the world to deliberate on how they can effectively work together to enhance the economy of their various countries was quite evident during the above forum.

The Forum provided opportunity for women entrepreneurs all over the world to share practical real experiences with each other. The Investment Forum was held simultaneously with the trade fair to expose women entrepreneurs to ways of enhancing their current businesses or creating new ones. Topics discussed during the workshops ranged from the role of women entrepreneurs in the enhancement of growth potential of the private sector to the use of technology to aid women businesses.

The conference recognised that the world economy is moving towards what others have termed 'global village' where boundaries would be nonexistent. Already, the World Trade Organisation has an ambitious plan to implement the trading partners such as the EEC, NAFTA, ASEAN, CARICOM and others are being formed to facilitate trade between nations. Globalisation also means that products from everywhere are being measured by the same standards. Moreover, the rapid development in information technology such as the Internet has meant that those who already have better access to lucrative markets are poised to strengthen their hold on such markets by sheer speed of communication.

Implications of the Uruguay Round

The Uruguay Round is the latest and most comprehensive in a series of global efforts to stimulate world trade by reducing both tariff and non-tariff barriers. According to Dr William F. Steel, Private Sector Development Adviser at the World Bank, who presented a paper on 'The New Global Environment for Trade: The implications of the Uruguay Round', the growing world trade can bring tremendous benefits to all countries by greatly expanding market opportunities and making goods available at the least possible cost. He emphasized that the spectacular growth of many Asian countries has been driven in large part by capturing a growing share of the expanding export markets.

However, the global market place keeps changing, and many countries are also concerned about protecting their domestic producers from these changes. Tariffs and restrictions imposed by these countries would make it difficult for new exporters to enter the market. Unfortunately, the biggest losers to these barriers are non-traditional exports from Africa.

Discussions, under the auspices of the World Trade Organisation, succeeded in gaining widespread agreements to reduce tariff levels, eliminate a lot of non-tariff restrictions, and remove various subsidies and special preferences in order to make trade more open and equal for everyone.

Loss of Preferential Markets

The concern among African countries is the loss of preferences granted to many of their exports that enter Europe under the Loire Convention. The Uruguay Round will trim such duty-free concessions. Europe and many other industrialised countries may be free to purchase goods from anywhere in the world without any obligation to buy goods from Africa. However, participants were reminded that the impact will be minimal because the maximum loss will be less than three percentage points from the current level. In addition, enormous gain will be realised in the other areas of the agreements.

Boost in Exports

The Uruguay Round is expected to boost world trade by as much as 10–15 per cent. This is a boon for women exporters. Participants were thus urged to take advantage of the increase in expanded world trade to help improve their businesses as well as boost their respective national economies.

Impact of Technology on Women's Businesses

Participants observed that there are tremendous opportunities for the development of exports within the globalised world economy, however, developing countries aiming to enter the world market would first have to tackle the technological gap that exists between them and the developed nations.

To facilitate entry of their products into the globalised market in the 21st century, women entrepreneurs would have to move away from the traditional marketing and production methods which often result in low productivity and substandard quality and adopt new technologies which will enable them to compete effectively.

According to Ms M. Chatrapathy, Women in Development Advisor of the Asian and Pacific Center for Transfer of Technology in India, there is the need for rural women to be equipped with the appropriate technologies as an alternative to traditional methods. Traditional methods, she pointed out are labour intensive and as a result often generate low returns. Food surpluses are often wasted because women do not have access to technologies that would allow them to process and store them. As a result, women food producers are often displaced by firms using latest technologies or imported materials.

Ms Shade Bembatoun-Young, an ECOWAS consultant, emphasised that to enable women entrepreneurs to effectively compete in the world market there is a need for rapid technological advancement in the various stages of the export business, such as processing, packaging and handling. This she said was particularly important because in the new global market place, products from everywhere will be measured by the same quality standards. For example, it is increasingly required that products carry the eco-label certifying that their production was not ecologically harmful.

According to Mrs Saba Mebrahtu of Eritrea, it is important for successful women entrepreneurs to actively support the upgrading of technologies, particularly those used by the informal sector where most women entrepreneurs operate.

Mrs Joyce Mapoma, Chairman of the Village Industry Service in Lusaka, Zambia, called for the technical skills of producers to be continually enhanced to meet the quality standards of the world market. She urged professionals, especially engineers, to find ways of applying new technology to the women dominated small-scale sector so as to improve on operational efficiency.

Participants were of the view that technology holds the key to Africa's economic growth within the global economy, particularly with regard to women's economic activities which tend to require improvement in product quality and productivity in order to compete globally.

Information Technology and Communication Networks to Enhance Women's Businesses and their Entrepreneurial Capabilities

Participants recognised that in Ghana, GAWE and the Association of Women in the Media had made a commendable headway in this regard, as practically demonstrated by the publication of a daily newspaper, 'Women Entrepreneurs' throughout the duration of the fair and investment forum.

However, the generally underdeveloped nature of communication networks in Africa presents one of the biggest challenges to women entrepreneurs. Governments must set up efficient communication infrastructure to facilitate trade. In order to gain access to market information as well as to world markets, women entrepreneurs were urged to establish good communication networks among themselves.

Dr Wakeelah Mutazammik, a communication expert from Malaysia, stressed the importance of communication links for the export sector to facilitate networking and information sharing.

Capacity Building for Women Entrepreneurs

The investment forum emphasised the need to develop the capacities of women entrepreneurs to compete effectively in the global market. To achieve this objective, there is a need to focus on the following:

- training and education;
- access to credit and women's banking;
- capacity building.

Training and Education

The importance of training and education was continually stressed throughout the Investment Forum as essential for the development of women's enterprises. This is because cultural biases and attitudes have conditioned women to 'think small' and have contributed to their lack of initiative to start and develop big businesses.

According to Mrs Akande from Nigeria, women need to be thoroughly groomed on how to prepare bankable proposals and what is required to qualify for loans. For instance, women seeking credit need to know the requirements of loan review boards such as local content (i.e. non-dependency on imports), export potential, the management team of the company and the level of equity contribution. Entrepreneurs build equity by saving money or owning land which can be used as collateral.

Women need to do their homework on issues such as packaging for export and should be well informed about the export business. Women entrepreneurs should be encouraged to join societies and form groups to apply for larger loans and collectively guarantee loan repayment for their members. Women entrepreneurs need to cultivate mutual confidence and trust among each other. Often some projects can not be done by a single woman entrepreneur and a joint venture is the best alternative. It was also stressed that women entrepreneurs need to access local and global information sources. Information on conducting market studies to information on technologies such as computers and Internet. GAWE was commended for using these new communication technology to send information globally about the Fair.

There was a need to demystify technical concepts such as feasibility studies, business plans and financial statements to make them more understandable. Women also need to be thoroughly groomed on how to technically prepare these essential business documents.

The importance of education was illustrated by an Eritrean woman who talked about how the ravages of war left her with a spouse in jail and insufficient funds to pay her staff pharmacist. Determined to keep her family together, she enrolled in a pharmacy programme, gained a diploma and maintained her business.

Access to Credit and Women's Banking

The crucial role of women's access to credit was a recurring theme throughout the Investment Forum.

According to Mrs Akande, only 10 per cent of total world credit goes to women although most financial institutions are equal opportunity lenders. This illustrates the importance of increasing women's access to credit if their enterprises are to grow. She further called on women entrepreneurs to improve their ability to access credit through training to be able to compete effectively for business financing rather than expect financial institutions to set substandard loan conditions. However, according to Obaapanyin Ama Yeboaa, Deputy Governor of the Bank of Ghana, a study by the UN Economic Commission for Africa (UNECA) in 1993 on the possibility of creating a bank for African women revealed that although lending mechanisms existed in African commercial banks the collateral requirement makes it difficult for women to qualify for credit.

The recommendations of the study therefore included:

- the need for an institution that would operate somewhere between a consumer finance company and an investment bank in order to minimise the currently strict limitations imposed on banks;
- the need for innovation in reaching out to women;
- the need to be profit oriented and self supporting;
- the need for women to take ownership of the bank.

Women's Associations

The Investment Forum recognised the need to strengthen the capacity of women's associations and networks. In a presentation on the challenges facing indigenous business associations in the 21st century, Mrs Haile of Ethiopia decried the major constraints facing indigenous associations:

- a lack of clarity of vision;
- lack of popular participation;
- lack of leadership skills;
- lack of organisational structure; and
- a lack of networking.

In her opinion, associations need to be well organised to act together for a common goal. She stressed that African regional and sub-regional economic bodies and business federations have a crucial role to play by strengthening the national associations of women entrepreneurs.

Conclusion

The Forum generated many useful ideas and suggestions for the ways in which the Ghanaian Association of Woman Entrepreneurs can move forward. The central importance of women's access to credit emerged out of a number of contributions made at the Forum. Similarly, the need for strengthening women's banking and women's organisations also emerged out of the discussions. The relevance of new technical forms such as the Internet to women's economic activities was also noted.

Note

1   Editors' note: the Forum was widely advertised on large billboards with strong visual displays thus giving high public visibility on gender and business issues.

8 Leading the Legal Battle: Gender Rights in Ghana

MRS REBECCA OSEI-BOATENG
ADMINISTRATOR, FIDA GHANA

Introduction

The Concise Oxford Dictionary, seventh edition, defines ' battle' as 'the struggle for one's rights'. Using the above definition, a legal battle is a struggle to ensure that one's legal rights are respected. In a country such as ours, where the Constitution (1992), Article 12 (2) provides that 'every person ... whatever his race, place of origin, political opinion, colour, religion, creed or gender shall be entitled to the fundamental human rights and freedoms of the individual', we can state for a fact that there are no laws in the statute books of Ghana which are overtly discriminatory against women.

In practice, however, women in Ghana have for centuries been denied the opportunities to participate on equal terms with their male counterparts in the political, social, economic, religious and cultural life of this country. Most Ghanaian women are: very poor, with very little education; they are usually employed in the informal sector, with very low incomes and they do not take part in major decisions affecting their lives.

The International Federation of Women Lawyers, Ghana Chapter (FIDA GHANA) was set up in 1974, by a group of female lawyers, with the aim of enhancing and promoting the welfare of women and children. Since 1985, FIDA GHANA has been engaged in a struggle to raise the consciousness of Ghanaian women to some of the injustices meted out to them by society through social, religious and customary practices such as widowhood rites, female genital mutilation and inheritance laws. FIDA GHANA Legal Services Centre offers the following services:

- legal aid clinic;
- legal aid literacy;
- advocacy.

Legal Aid Clinic

The Platform for Action, Fourth World Conference on Women, Beijing, 4–15 September 1995, identified the persistent and increasing burden of poverty on women as one of the critical areas of concern. Paragraph 58 (p) of the Platform for Action urges governments to 'ensure access to free or low-cost legal services'. A decade before Beijing, in 1985, FIDA GHANA realised that indigent Ghanaian women were facing a serious handicap in obtaining adequate legal representation in the courts because they could not afford the services of lawyers. FIDA GHANA therefore established a Legal Aid Programme, the first of its kind in Ghana. The Legal Aid Programme is aimed primarily at the poor and indigent women and children.

Members of FIDA GHANA render voluntary service in the form of counselling, mediation and legal advice. The number of cases handled at the Legal Aid Clinic has increased steadily each year from 47 cases in 1985 to 1047 in 1995.

Table 8.1   Total number of cases and categories (1995)

Classification	No.	Percentage
Maintenance	434	41.45
Estate	180	17.19
Access to children	137	13.09
Family	148	14.14
Divorce	62	5.92
Property	40	3.82
Breach of promise to marry	17	1.62
Criminal	9	0.86
Labour	8	0.76
Tort	7	0.67
Other	5	0.48
Total	1,047	100.00

Source: FIDA GHANA 1995 Annual Report.

An analysis of the above table shows that 41.45 per cent of the cases handled at the Legal Aid Clinic relate to the maintenance of children. Although Ghanaian fathers have a legal responsibility to maintain their children under the Maintenance of Children's Decree 1977 (SMCD 133) some fathers just refuse to maintain their children, leaving the children's mothers to shoulder the financial responsibility of bringing up such children single-handedly. Through the intervention of FIDA GHANA, fathers who are brought to the Legal Aid Centre are made, through mediation, to make monthly payments for the food, education and medical expenses of their children. In cases of recalcitrant fathers, the cases are sent to the family tribunals where members of FIDA GHANA represent the children's mothers free of charge. The second category of cases commonly handled by FIDA GHANA relate to estate matters. Widows and children are assisted to benefit from the estate of their deceased husbands and fathers, under the Intestate Succession Law, 1985 (PNDCL 111).

In January 1997, FIDA GHANA opened an office in Kumasi to cater for clients in the Northern sector of the country, that is Ashanti, Brong Ahafo, Upper East, Upper West and the Northern regions. In addition to the regular legal aid clinics run from its offices in Accra and Kumasi, FIDA GHANA periodically organises mobile Legal Aid Clinics in towns close to its two offices. At such mobile clinics, rural women are given an opportunity to discuss their legal problems with a team of lawyers. Files are opened for individuals whose cases need further examination. Clients are subsequently requested to call at FIDA GHANA offices in Accra or Kumasi for follow up action. FIDA GHANA has organised mobile clinics in Nsawam, Amasaman, Akim Oda, Nkoranza, Obuasi and Offinso.

Legal Literacy

Work at the Legal Aid Centre and interaction of FIDA GHANA with thousands of women revealed the low level of literacy and ignorance amongst Ghanaian women about their rights under the law. There are two components of the legal literacy programme. The first component consists of seminars and workshops aimed at educating women on their legal rights and where to go for redress in case of breaches of these rights. The seminars are conducted in the local languages and FIDA GHANA tries to involve, through networking with various grassroots women groups, as wide a representation of women as possible to attend these seminars.

As part of its literacy programme, FIDA GHANA has adopted a Rights Awareness Programme under which seminars have been held for target groups such as queenmothers[1] and traditional rulers. FIDA GHANA has targeted queenmothers for the purposes of explaining to them the laws that affect the welfare of women and children, in the expectation that they will in turn explain these laws to members of their respective communities, thereby creating greater awareness of their rights and responsibilities.

In the Northern, Upper East and Upper West Regions of Ghana which do not have a system of queenmothers, FIDA GHANA has extended its Rights Awareness Programme to traditional rulers, conscious of the fact that if women and children are sensitised on their rights but traditional rulers and other opinion leaders are left out of the sensitisation programme, there is a danger that the old laws will continue to be applied, to the detriment of women and children.

The second component of the legal literacy programme covers the simplification and translation of the basic laws affecting the status of women. Under FIDA GHANA's 'Women and the Law' series, the following laws have been simplified and translated into four main local languages, namely Akan, Ewe, Ga and Dagbani:

- Intestate Succession Law, 1985 (PNDCL 111);
- Wills Act, 1971 (ACT 360);
- Marriage Laws;
- Maintenance of Children Decree (SMCD 133);
- Divorce Under the Matrimonial Causes (ACT 367);
- Administration of Estates.

The 'Women and the Law' series has reduced the laws involved in their simplest form, eliminating as far as possible all technical language so as to make the laws understandable and accessible to all sections of the reading public.

Advocacy

The FIDA GHANA Advocacy programme involves promoting the review and reform of laws and traditional practices that tend to negate the status of women. Article 26 (2) of the 1992 Constitution states: 'All customary practices which dehumanise or are injurious to the physical and mental well-being of a person are prohibited'. It is common knowledge, however, that in several Ghanaian communities women are made to undergo inhuman widowhood rites on the pretext that custom demands such rites on the death of a husband. Certain communities practice female genital mutilation (FGM) although the Criminal Code (Amendment) Act, 1994 (Act 484) makes the practice of FGM a second degree felony, punishable by a term of imprisonment of not less than three years. In 1990, due to intense lobbying and advocacy by women's groups including FIDA GHANA, Criminal Code (Amendment) Law 1984 (PNDCL 90) was passed, which was an amendment of section 88 A (1) of the Criminal Code of Ghana. This amendment makes the perpetuation of cruel widowhood rites a misdemeanour and seeks to punish those who engage in inhuman practices such as throwing pepper in the eyes of widows, the tying of ropes around widows, shaving of widows' hair or obliging widows to sleep on the floor for 40 days.

FIDA GHANA has done much to promote the above laws and familiarise Ghanaian women with their respective rights under the law. FIDA GHANA played a leading role in promoting the review of the following four laws, namely:

- Intestate Succession Law, 1985 (PNDCL 111);
- Customary Marriage and Divorce (Registration) Law 1985 (PNDCL 112);
- Administration of Estates (Amendment) Law 1985 (PNDCL 113);
- The Head of Family Accountability by Law, 1985 (PNDCL 114).

PNDCL 111 sought to apportion to widows and children a greater share of the estate on the death intestate of a husband and father. PNDCL 112 provides for the registration of customary marriages. PNDCL 113 effected changes in the law relating to the administration of Estates to take account of the rights of widows and children under the Intestate Succession Law. PNDCL 114 obliges a head of family to account for any family property in his possession.

Paragraph 60 (f) of the Platform for Action urges national and international non-governmental organisations and women's groups to 'mobilise to protect women's right to full and equal access to economic resources, including the right to inheritance and to ownership of land and other property ...'. Through its legal aid programme, FIDA GHANA is assisting women and children to claim their due share of the estates of their deceased husbands and fathers.

In 1993, FIDA GHANA took up the issue of the 'Trokosi' or the vestal virgins system practised in some parts of the Volta Region. 'Trokosi' is a custom whereby virgin females are made to serve fetish priests/priestesses as a pacification to the gods for an offence committed by a member of their family. FIDA GHANA in a presentation on the 'Legal basis for the abolition of the Trokosi system' has raised two basic questions about the 'Trokosi' system:

- why should only females be made to serve 'life sentences' in these shrines for crimes committed by the relations who are often males?
- of what use does it serve a country for an innocent person to be punished?

Through the intervention of the Commission on Human Rights and Administrative Justice, the National Commission for Civic Education and non governmental organisations such as FIDA GHANA and International Needs, a number of these vestal virgins have been set free. It is the hope of FIDA GHANA that parliament will see its way clear to put an end to the dehumanising aspects of the 'Trokosi' system.

FIDA GHANA has also advocated that other laws affecting the status of women be looked at, especially in the area of violence against women. FIDA GHANA has prepared a draft handbook on domestic violence in Ghana as a guide for victims of violence as well as those who deal with victims of violence. It is hoped that this handbook would contribute towards the elimination of gender based violence in Ghana. FIDA GHANA would like to see the passage of legislation dealing with intra family offences.

FIDA GHANA is also advocating for the repeal of section 42 (g) of the criminal code which states that consent given by a husband or wife at marriage for the purpose of marriage cannot be revoked until the partners are divorced or separated by a judgement of a competent court. This provision lays down the general proposition that there is no such thing as 'rape' within the context of marital relations. Thus forced sex within marriage does not constitute an offence either under customary or statutory law in Ghana.

FIDA GHANA is also advocating that action should be taken to comply with Article 22 (2) and (3) of the 1992 constitution. This article states that parliament should, as soon as practicable, enact legislation governing the property rights of spouses.

Conclusion

The legal battle for gender rights in Ghana is a long and arduous one. Any exercise which involves changing the mentality, attitudes, customs and culture of people and communities needs a lot of patience and perseverance. FIDA GHANA can however say with pride that it has succeeded in raising the consciousness of the Ghanaian woman to some of the injustices of gender inequalities, her rights under the constitution and the laws of Ghana and instilled in her the confidence to take steps to enforce those rights.

70   *Maintaining the Momentum of Beijing*

FIDA GHANA is most grateful for the assistance received from donor agencies such as the United States Agency for International Development, Fredreich Ebert Foundation, Canadian High Commission, Dunchurch Aid and German Women World Day of Prayer. FIDA GHANA has been able to fulfil its aims and objectives largely through the kind assistance and generous donations of these donor agencies.

Note

1   Editors' note : 'Queenmother' is a customary position of authority occupied by women in Ghana – the queenmother of a community would have influence over its choice of male leader. In the present, 'queenmothers' are also found in the commercial sphere within local markets where they coordinate women's trading activities, most particularly in terms of setting prices.

9 Keeping Connected and Moving Forward: The Importance of New Technology

PROFESSOR NANA ARABA APT
DIRECTOR OF CENTRE FOR SOCIAL POLICY STUDIES, GHANA
AND DR NAANA AGYEMANG-MENSAH
GENDER SPECIALIST, ASSID, GHANA

Introduction

In Ghana presently, Beijing has become a cliché synonymous with woman power, woman ability, woman leadership, in short woman empowerment. Annoying as it is sometimes to hear 'Beijing' any time a female does the unexpected or on the contrary a male does not want to do the expected, one message clearly stands out in this Ghana example that there is at least among the general populace, an awareness of the imminent change in the status of women. The need to keep this momentum going is obvious. The wheels of change are in motion and it is up to women to ensure that the motion continues unabated. One way of ensuring this momentum is to make it possible for more women to participate in decisions that affect them, their families and their communities. Recently, a woman director of an NGO working with rural women in Ghana was interviewed in a Ghanaian weekly newspaper (*Public Agenda*, 18–22 June 1997). She told of a pattern she had encountered a number of times when village committees had to be set up.

> When it came to choosing leaders, everywhere they said the committees should have a male head. But if you suggested a woman to head committees, they said 'oh yes of course', it's like it escaped the whole community both men and women that women can play a leading role in the activities of the community' (*Public Agenda*, p. 8).

71

Given the prevalence of attitudes which see women as less capable than men, or that women have to be led by men, both women and men have to be sensitised to ensure that obstacles are removed in the way of women's participation in decision-making. One way to remove stumbling blocks is for women themselves to work to move themselves forward instead of waiting to be appreciated.

Database: Women Helping Women Grow

Education has been found to provide a tool for enhancing one's capability, economically, socially and politically. Empowerment of women is indeed an essential factor in ensuring their effective participation in development. Thus the need for economic and for political empowerment could be achieved through education and training and by involving women in the decision-making process. NGOs and community-level organisations have a particular role to play in assisting in the empowerment process.

Although a number of women in Africa are hard-working, resourceful and doing well in business, yet a lot more could do better given the right kind of education and training. In the informal sector, where many African women operate, a stumbling block is surely the lack of sufficient know-how and expertise for entrepreneurship. The main problems which face women in this sector include lack of managerial skills, high illiteracy rate and lack of credit facilities. Consequently, many women continue to use traditional methods to operate their businesses. Professional women as well as women's organisations should therefore prioritise the agenda of making literacy education accessible to women of all ages and ensuring their participation. A way to do this across cultures and regional boundaries is through the Internet: to create a web page that enables idea sharing and cost sharing among professional African women and gender organisations and thus helping develop the capabilities of those handicapped by lack of education or training.

In order to integrate women into development, it will be important to develop and maintain long-term and short-term strategies which will demonstrate the productive capacity and contribution of women. The income-generating project approach is an appropriate strategy. Creating and expanding access to credit facilities is essential to this approach. Getting women connected and helping each other in their activities is a catalyst approach.

An appropriate information network, covering research, existing data sources, projects and programmes and existing organisations and funding sources, is essential to the process of integrating women into mainstream development. As a first step, the focal points in a network of African women for development should be identified and organised to receive basic sets of available national and regional data. Network participants should ensure that any information they produce or receive is shared with other network members and end users, that is, women themselves.

In an effort to promote gender networking, in collaborative projects, and at various fora organised by African women professionals and women's organisations, a concerted effort must be made to reduce the cost of locating women participants. One way to do this is to create a central database of women scholars, policy-makers, and development practitioners which would be accessible to all African regions. Such a database would provide a pool of women participants from which to recruit candidates for internal and regional network, as well as for participation in a wide range of activities aimed to promote the social and economic well-being of women in particular, the unskilled and the uneducated.

Management of the Database

Costs associated with the provision and maintenance of such a database through the network could be very high. Instead, for ease of management and to lower costs, it is recommended that such a database be located in one country. Given appropriate funding, the Centre for Social Policy Studies (CSPS), at the University of Ghana, could offer such a facility on its already developed web page to be located under its gender activities heading. One or two staff members can be trained in its use, and will be responsible for updating records, and meeting requests for information. Though simple, the database will be powerful enough to enable selection of names based on a number of criteria, for example area of expertise, academic discipline, or regional interest. This will enable names to be easily pulled out and provided to those requesting them.

Compiling the Database

The usefulness of such a database depends on its content. There is a tremendous amount of information on women scholars and professionals in Africa but this is located in different organisations in different countries. Compiling all names in a central database would be of benefit to all.

A successful database will provide enough relevant information for planning purposes. It is envisioned that only fields for which information is consistently available will be maintained. In this way, the database will not create expectations for information it can not deliver.

The following initial fields are suggested. Some of these may have multiple options:

- name;
- institutional affiliation;
- position;
- academic qualifications;
- academic discipline;
- disciplinary specialisation;
- institutional address;
- telephone number;
- fax/telex number;
- Internet address;
- country of origin;
- citizenship;
- primary geographic area of interest;
- secondary geographic area of interest;
- primary field of interest;
- secondary field of interest;
- affiliation with formal network/organisations/institutes.

Database Software

Computer services will be asked to assist in the selection of a software package which is powerful, user-friendly and manageable in the Windows environment. Maintenance of the database will be the responsibility of one institution in one country.

Conclusion

It is hoped that armed with the relevant information, gender NGOs will be better able to integrate more women scholars into their research, outreach and training activities. It is recognised that simply providing information is not enough to improve gender activities, but it is a necessary first step.

The fact that resources for development in Africa are limited should not prevent the concerns of women from being integrated into existing development projects and programmes. Multilateral, bilateral and financial lending institutions and assistance agencies should be encouraged to include this concern in the guidelines for preparing projects that benefit women and as a criterion in project approval. The participation of women in the preparation of development programmes, and in political processes should be encouraged and what better means presently offer such opportunities than through the electronic media? Creating and expanding such technological facilities is essential for the connectivity of women and their strides to empowerment.

Education is an essential factor in the advancement of women as well as influencing the potential contribution of women to development both for existing women and for future generations of women in Africa. Recognition of the importance of women's potential and a departure from the emphasis on problems leading to vulnerability, is a major factor for the integration of women in development. Therefore in all African countries, a major effort should be made to ensure access of all women to basic education, to information on development processes, to learning skills (both traditional and non-traditional) and to retraining, where necessary.

PART 2
VOICES FROM AFRICAN WOMEN – EXPERTS IN OUR OWN DEVELOPMENT, PARTICIPANTS IN OUR FUTURE

10 The Political Empowerment of Women: Constraints to their Participation and Strategies to Increase it

HONOURABLE MIRIA MATEMBE
MEMBER OF PARLIAMENT, UGANDA

Introduction

At the 5th Africa Regional Conference on Women held in Dakar, Senegal 16–23 November 1994, the *African Platform for Action* identified 11 critical areas of concern for the advancement of women for peace, equality and development. Fortunately, almost all these critical areas of concern for African women were incorporated into the Beijing Platform for Action. One of these issues was the *political empowerment* of women, prioritised as the seventh area of concern.

It was clearly established that there is a low level of representation in the political decision-making process by African women: the need to increase the level of women's political participation was seen as an imperative since unless women participate in the shaping of structures and influencing decisions and policies which affect their lives, their situation can never improve. Politics is the centre of power, and power is the key to women's advancement.

It is against this background that 'The Voices from African Women Initiative' contracted me to conduct a networking exercise with African women in order to identify factors which constrain women from participating in politics and to explore views of African women on measures which can be taken to empower them politically.

I carried on this exercise between February and April 1996. I networked both regionally and nationally. Regionally, I participated in a seminar organised for the African Women in Decision-making held at Kampala. This seminar brought together women politicians from Kenya, Tanzania, Ethiopia, Eritrea, Rwanda, Ghana, Uganda and Zimbabwe.

I also organised a workshop for Ugandan women politicians at national and local levels which brought together women from Rukungiri, Kabale, Kisoro, Ntungamo, Bushenyi and Mbarara. Both these meetings extensively discussed the issue of African women's political empowerment. They identified constraints and suggested measures to remedy the situation.

The issue of women's political participation was looked at from two aspects, namely

- women participants as candidates to elective posts, and
- women participants as voters.

Although there are constraints which are unique to women at local levels of participation, the participants at regional and local levels were in agreement as to the major constraints.

It was observed at both meetings that although African women have made entry into the political arena, this entry has been limited to increasing numbers of women entering the system but has not yet affected the political agenda to reflect the broad concerns of the women. The dominant agenda still favours men.

Constraints to African Women's Political Participation

Lack of Peaceful and Conducive Environment

Africa has been, and many parts of it continues to be, a place of internal conflict and civil strife, circumstances which make it difficult for women to participate in politics. Under such conditions, politics have been regarded as a 'dirty game' in which women and other good-minded people can not participate. Besides, in such conditions, women's issues are relegated to the back of the political agenda because human survival becomes the primary goal.

Lack of Political Will on the Part of African Governments

It was observed that political will on the part of government is very crucial to women's political participation. Countries like Uganda and South Africa were seen as examples of governments whose political will has made it possible for women to participate. However, even in many African countries where there are no upheavals, governments have not given the necessary political will. Countries like Kenya, Zimbabwe and Zambia were mentioned.

Structures and Systems

It was noted that the existing political structures and systems are not responsive to women's participation. In their attempts to participate in these structures, women have found themselves 'swallowed up'. Many have just decided to fit in the structures and play the usual roles played by men, thus endorsing the oppressive and exploitative systems.

Customs and Cultural Practices

It was agreed that Africans cherish certain customs and cultural practices which are oppressive and relegate women to a position of inferiority and regard them as minors, incapable of managing their own affairs and making independent decisions affecting their lives. Such customs and cultural practices and attitudes have contributed to lack of economic independence on the part of women.

Poverty Among Women

Poverty among women is a big hindrance to their political participation. Politics is a very expensive venture. For women to contest elections, especially at high levels like national parliaments and regional posts within their countries, they need a lot of money to spend on campaigns. Politics in Africa is very different from developed countries because the electorate is not influenced by the ability and competence of the candidate but by what the candidate is able to offer in terms of basic needs of the people. During campaigns, voters expect provision of handouts like sugar, soap, school fees for their children and the like. Men are able to raise money either from their wealth since they own property, or from their wealthy colleagues, an advantage which women do not enjoy.

High Levels of Illiteracy Among African Women

Because in Africa illiteracy levels are very high and the situation is worse among women because when it comes to education, boys are given priority since they are culturally viewed as superior to girls, this means that women can not offer themselves as candidates, nor can they effectively participate as voters.

There is also lack of political awareness among women, caused mainly by lack of political interest because women have been looking at politics as an occupation for the men only.

Lack of Skills

It was noted that even where women have come up to participate, their participation has not been effective because they lack political skills. Men have been in this game for so long and many have learned through experience. Women need political skills like the art of public speaking, confidence, lobbying, advocacy, networking, organisation and the like to be able to compete with these experts.

Inadequate and Discriminatory Laws

The African countries got their inherited laws from their former colonisers. Many of these laws, despite their being obsolete, have continued to exist on the statute books and constrain women from attaining equality and political participation. Where gaps do exist, Africans resort to culture which is the biggest offender in the violation of women's rights.

Lack of Modernisation

Lack of modernisation and proper infrastructure in Africa was identified as a big constraint especially for women's participation in politics at lower levels. In a situation where social services are very poor and inadequate, where there is no appropriate technology to ease the women's workload, women have very little time or no time at all to participate in politics. They are basically preoccupied with the survival of their families and they have not been able to relate politics to the problems of their daily life.

Due to lack of political awareness many Africans, especially women, have not been able to understand the relevance of politics to their everyday life. Therefore, women would rather spend their time on their heavy workload than go to attend seminars and workshops for political empowerment.

These, and other factors, like intrigue among women, emphasis of non-issues, lack of support for each other, were identified as factors which hinder women's participation in politics.

Strategies to Improve the Situation

The African women involved in the networking on political empowerment identified the following as strategies to help increase their participation in politics.

Peaceful Environment

There is a need for Africa to get itself rid of wars. For this, women suggest their involvement in peace missions and other structures which have been established for conflict resolution. Women have continuously been left out of these structures and yet it is women and mothers of our nations who know how to talk the language of peace.

Women suggest that it would be useful if a team of prominent African women were constituted to work on conflict resolution by visiting countries and warring factions and talking to leaders about the need for peace.

National Machineries and Application of Affirmative Action

Establishment and strengthening of national machineries for the advancement of women and application of affirmative action were identified as good strategies. For these two strategies to work, women must harness the political will of their governments. Such machineries must be properly financed and be headed by people who are gender sensitive and responsive to the needs of women.

In many countries where such machineries exist, they are just relegated to the back yard as a formality and have not achieved their expected goals. On the issue of affirmative action, which involves policies to appoint women on high decision-making levels, women suggested as a measure that it should not just be any women to be appointed but those women who are familiar with women's issues and committed to women's advancement. Therefore, women should have say in the appointment of their fellow women to political positions. They recommend a committee of highly qualified and committed women to act as an advisory body to governments in the appointment of women. The quarter system for parliamentary and local council seats was also seen as a very important measure. It has worked to motivate many women to join politics. The Uganda case was cited as a glaring example.

Structural Transformation

Transformation of existing structures and systems to make them women-friendly was also seen as a measure to increase women's participation in politics.

Gender Sensitisation

Gender sensitisation of society to make it gender sensitive was also said to be a strategy. This would help to demystify the roles played by men/boys in society. It would also help society to know the potentials, talents and wisdom of women so as to be able to change the biased cultural attitudes of society towards women. Coupled with gender sensitisation was modernisation as a strategy. With improved technology, men can help in playing the roles hitherto seen as a preserve for women.

Men could easily help in the domestic chores if there were modern equipment like cookers rather than firewood and charcoal stoves. This would go a long way in reducing the women's heavy workload which denies them the opportunity to participate in public life.

Women Role Models

Women who have become successful in politics should act as role models so as to motivate others to take interests in politics. Exemplary performance in leadership can raise the interest of young women.

Training Centres

Establishment of training centres for political and economic skills development is a necessary strategy.

Support Funds

Establishment of organisations or systems of fund-raising to support women politicians financially is another important strategy. Women have to learn to support each other financially like men do. The 'EMILY'S LIST' fund in Washington was cited as a good example of such a system.

Trade and business

Women need to get interested in trade both nationally and regionally, because unless there are big businesswomen to generate income, women would not be able to assist fellow women politicians. Ghana women were cited as examples of women who have excelled in business and trade.

Women's Political Agenda

As a strategy, women need to develop a specific political agenda. They need to broaden networks and build alliances across regions so as to exchange knowledge, learn what is happening in other nations and regions, what has worked there and see how they can apply the same to their situations in their nations. Networks like the East African Women Parliamentarians Association which has been formed are important for women's political empowerment. A country like Kenya can learn from its neighbour Uganda about the importance and relevance of affirmative action in increasing women's participation in politics. Women politicians must link up with NGOs for support.

Unity of Purpose

It was also agreed as a strategy that women should be able to unite on women's issues and vote across party lines. Only when women have a common united front will they influence laws and policies to their needs.

Civic Education

Political awareness creation and political skills development for grassroots women to enable them to participate in voting and contesting for local councils is very important. Women need to know the power they have in their numbers and to be able to use it to vote fellow women and gender sensitive men into power.

Prioritisation of Issues

Prioritisation of issues and important projects to carry on for political empowerment of women was also seen as a good strategy.

Political Associations

Women politicians should form effective national women politicians' associations through which they can build and support each other, learn each other's different skills and talents, and be able to employ these skills and talents as and when necessary. This would help to minimise antagonism, envy and conflicts that tend to be more pronounced among women than men.

Media

Knowledge and use of mass media was also identified as a strategy to increase women's political participation. Media can either destroy or build up a politician.

Constitutional and Legal Reform

Constitutional and legal reforms were identified as a big measure to increase women's participation in politics. Law can be an effective instrument for women's advancement. It was noted with gratification that some African countries like South Africa, Eritrea, Ethiopia and Uganda have taken advantage of the democratisation process that has been going on in Africa to effect constitutional reforms which have not only done away with discrimination against women but have also made provisions for guaranteeing, promoting and protecting women's rights. The Uganda case is a very good one.

Conclusion

All this said and done, it is extremely crucial for Africa as a continent to become economically and politically independent. Africa needs to design political systems and structures which are appropriate and suitable to its people to be able to enjoy real democracy. Democracy and effective political participation are but a sham in a continent besieged by abject poverty and high levels of illiteracy. Africa has to break away from enslavement.

11 Grassroots Women's Initiatives to Overcome Poverty: A Report of Eastern Africa Networking Experience

WINIFRED CHEGE
COUNCIL FOR THE ECONOMIC EMPOWERMENT OF WOMEN IN AFRICA, KENYA

Introduction

Women believe that if they were in control there would be less hunger, less wastage of national resources, less conflict and better quality of life. Their contribution to country economies and maintenance of the family under very difficult circumstances is further confirmation of this belief. This understanding is the outcome of a three month dialogue with women groups, individual women, policy-makers and implementers in Kenya, Ethiopia, Uganda and Namibia.[1] In this chapter, I have summarised the economic situation of women at the African grassroots and their perception of Structural Adjustment Programmes (SAPs) as well as their effect on their lives. I have also highlighted women's efforts to mobilise for survival and to overcome poverty.

This chapter focuses on poverty reduction and women's initiatives to mobilise savings and access credit in groups and the effect of SAPs on grassroots women. It also recounts the effects of economic policies on women, and emphasises the need to support women's initiative at the grassroots through the trickle up approach.

Other than a networking tool, this report will form the basis for strategic planning to support grassroots associations by Council for the Economic Empowerment of Women in Africa (CEEWA) and Federation of Grassroots Women Associations of Kenya (FEGWAK), the organisations that participated in this dialogue.

Recent Developments

The rate of economic illiteracy among women is incredible. Both the educated and the uneducated consider economic issues to be the preserve of men. As a result economic issues are not given the attention they deserve. Several initiatives and opportunities at the national and regional as well as international levels that could benefit women go unexploited. But there are signs of change. It is only a few weeks ago that women representatives from 13 African countries networking on economic empowerment issues were exposed to the existence of the SPA programme (Special Programme of Assistance for Highly Indebted Low Income Countries of Sub-Saharan Africa). The experiences of the writer through the said CEEWA/WIDE Consultation on SPA enriched this chapter.

Current Situation of Women

Throughout modern history women have mobilised themselves in various forms to respond to the pressing social, cultural, economic, religious and political needs of the time. At the same time needs fulfilment has been a cardinal preoccupation of the African woman because of the multiple role they play in production, reproduction and community management.

Despite the enormous contribution of African women towards the development of nations, which has belatedly and grudgingly been recognised, they continue to suffer under the yoke of poverty because of enormous constraining factors which they face. Yet women spend most of their best energies striving to overcome poverty. It is an established fact, for instance, that women form the vast majority of the world's poorest poor. It was for this reason that 'Women and Poverty' was brought out as a major theme in the African Global Platform for Action (APFA) developed in Dakar in 1994 as part of the preparatory process for the Fourth United Nations World Conference on Women in Beijing, China in 1995 which also adopted the poverty theme.

The struggle for alleviation of widespread poverty presents the most daunting challenge to the African women. It is, however, encouraging that women have not resigned to this predicament. Everywhere in Africa, women are generating innovative and imaginative initiatives to overcome poverty. But like most other areas of national life, these heroic initiatives have not been documented. It is for this reason that the Voices from African Women initiative (VAW) has taken the lead to collate these innovations and develop a network so that efforts may be disseminated to benefit increased numbers of struggling women to attract attention of policy-makers on the effect of their actions on poor women.

Poverty Reduction Initiatives

The poverty web in which women are entangled is reinforced by the wholesale application of social-economic policies which impact negatively on marginalised groups. Such policies are implemented without involving those people they are likely to deprive. A case in point is the implementation of the Structural Adjustment Programmes (SAPs) which were aggressively promoted by the World Bank and the International Monetary Fund (IMF) in a bid to resuscitate the national economies but without apparent safety nets for the poor and the marginalised. The net effect of SAPs was reduction in public spending in social sectors such as food security, health and education, increase in bank interest rates, and redundancies in the civil service among others. Grassroots communities, especially women, have borne the brunt of SAPs, yet they have not been consulted.

Existing Situation

The following is the existing situation with regard to poverty reduction.

* There is widespread poverty among the vast majority of women manifested in lack of access to economic resources, low literacy levels, poor health, low income levels, poor nutrition and housing. The incidence of poverty is unequal across the social, gender and rural/urban divide. Women are virtually absent from national and grassroots institutions at which resource decisions are made.
* There are several actions initiated at individual, grassroots, local, national and international level to assist women to overcome poverty. Initiatives at higher levels of intervention have a macro approach and therefore tend to have less than the desired impact whereas grassroots initiatives yield better results. Indeed, women have organised themselves into groups and associations throughout the continent to address their plight.
* Most grassroots women groups have been given official recognition by national governments but there is little evidence of appropriate legal instruments and programme support. Also lacking is government recognition and quantification of women's unpaid work. Economic data

analysis is gender biased and does not reflect the existing economic reality.

- Governments have failed to involve women and other vulnerable groups in the formulation, implementation and monitoring of economic programmes with the sobering effect of increased poverty. Social dimension development policies and programmes have come in too late and are inadequate. Women are still absent in their formulation and implementation.

Possible Solutions and Interventions

- Develop a model for quantifying women's and men's unpaid labour and lobby for the establishment of compensation schemes and inclusion into satellite accounts.
- Initiate strategies and schemes that maintain food security at the family level.
- Encourage and lobby for women's participation in economic decision-making structures at the grassroots level (cooperatives, relief and development committees) through positive discrimination. A ratio of 20/80 could be a starting point.
- Develop tools and mechanisms for monitoring anti-poverty programmes at country level.
- War is an economic issue and the Organisation for African Unity (OAU) should lobby national governments to propagate peaceful environments free from strife which retards development and misapplies resources thus increasing poverty.
- Labour saving technology appropriate for Africa should be made available at all levels. This should include more equal distribution of roles at the family level.
- Increase research and documentation of women's economic activities, especially savings and credit at the grassroots level and develop support schemes for these initiatives. A starting point could be the training of African women in economic gender analysis.

Savings Mobilisation and Access to Credit

Access to credit is crucial for investments. Investing in productive enterprises is an important contribution to poverty alleviation. Grassroots women, therefore, require to access credit to invest in economic viable enterprises in order to break away from the yoke of poverty.

Existing Situation

The following situation obtains in Africa in regard to access to credit.

- Grassroots women mobilise savings which they deposit with banks and financial institutions. Unfortunately the banks and financial institutions have not identified women as special beneficiary groups for credit. Lending institutions continue to make rigid collateral requirements, with complicated and complex documentation and gender insensitive banking hours. Consequently women are shut out of credit.
- There are several non-governmental organisations which have identified the credit access gap and are in the business of advancing credit to grassroots women. Such NGOs operate along the Grameen's Bank Model. The NGOs do a thriving business as repayment is very high and there is sufficient demand. Since the model under which they operate assumes the existence of a money lender their interest rates are higher than that of formal banks.
- The existing sources of credit fall far short of demand. Grassroots women would prefer credit which is devoid of excessive formal requirements, accompanied by complementary services and initially advanced on concessionary terms.
- Access to credit is conditioned by ownership of assets such as land, buildings, machinery, capital market instruments and livestock. The global picture is that women own only one per cent of the world's assets. The average is much lower for Africa where most inheritance of assets is patriarchal.
- Women groups have perfected credit advancing to their members as a central activity of their existence. Credit programmes which are styled as 'merry-go-round' and other packages constitute the most reliable form of credit. The loans may be advanced at full market rates or concessionary rates depending on the circumstances and the rules of the group. Repayment is high as there is collective arrangement to manage the credit.
- There is inadequate documentation, recognition and support of women initiatives to advance credit, yet the amounts so generated by far outstrip those generated by banks both in the numbers supported and the amounts advanced.

Possible Solutions and Interventions

- Intensively promote the proposed women's development bank with

channels for accessing credit to grassroots women.
- Lobby for increased utilisation of available funds in accessing credit to African women at the grassroots.
- Lobby banks and other financial institutions to develop women friendly credit programmes with flexible terms and timing. Governments on their part should declare explicit policy guidelines for accessing credit to the poor.
- Quantify savings and credit mobilised by grassroot associations and include them in national accounts.

Grassroots Women's Response to SAPs

Most of the key economic policies in Africa are linked to Structural Adjustment Programmes (SAPs). The SAPs were propagated by governments with all the attendant negative implications. Subsequent and belated attempts to build in social dimensions of development have not been felt at the grassroots. Major policy expositions by governments have not addressed alleviation of the negative impact of SAPs which has resulted in negative growth to those below the poverty line.

There is overwhelming evidence that grassroots women were devastated by the implementation of SAPs. The cost of living skyrocketed and the ability to afford food, shelter, health, clothing and education was severely eroded. The situation was exacerbated by lack of involvement of the vulnerable groups and failure to package appropriate safety nets.

Existing Situation

The overall situation relating to the implementation of the SAPs is as follows.

- The process towards the conception and implementation of SAPs left grassroots women more deprived in social and economic terms than before. The early years of SAPs implementation were especially difficult as women could barely afford the basic necessities of life.
- Women began to innovate activities to assist them to cope with the hardship resulting from the SAPs. Women's grassroot organisations changed from a social orientation to a more economic and political orientation. Some organisations which were already engaged in income-generating activities have changed to higher levels of sophistication.

- Grassroots women are aware of critical elements of SAPs that directly affect their lives including cost sharing in education and health care, privatisation of public corporations, withdrawal of food subsidies, relaxation of protectionism and retrenchment in the public sector employment. They are however at a loss as to the reasoning and the needs for SAPs.
- At the macro level there is loud talk about SAP safety nets but there is no evidence of budgetary or programme commitment.
- Retrenchment and civil service reform affects women more than men because of the lower cadres of employment they occupy. This has resulted in a significant increase in the number of women who have become entrepreneurs but they are still constrained by lack of certified markets and business management skills. Skills training and business start up capital (commonly known as the 'golden handshake') are inadequate to say the least.
- There are very few agencies which have evolved support programmes for grassroots women in response to SAPs. They put emphasis on self-sustainability of projects and avoidance of donor's dependency but are constrained by inability to conceptualise and package appropriate support.
- National institutions which are supposed to advocate the cause of women have not found a voice to lobby for inclusion of SAP safety nets in the national agenda. Most of them lack capacity to implement their mandate.

Possible Solutions and Interventions

- Increase women's participation in the design, implementation and monitoring of SAPs in order to give them a human face and reduce the negative effects.
- Agricultural support programmes should redirect emphasis from traditional cash crops which use women's free labour to food crops which enhance food security at the home and whose income women have control over.
- SAPs safety nets should apply the micro approach of implementation. Programmes to cushion the poor should be made visible and transparent at the grassroots.

Other Initiatives

In a bid to improve the performance of women undertaking individual or group activities, other interventions are necessary. These include:

Training Grassroots women have received some training for the improvement of general reproductive roles (family life, education and health) but performance in productive activities (business management, lobbying and negotiation) has received minimal support.

Technical assistance Some public and non-profit agencies have extended technical assistance to grassroots women. It is valued intervention but so little that it's like a drop of water in the sea.

Access to expanded markets Access to market remains a major constraint but a few women have adopted a more aggressive approach to marketing of their produce. The presence of women at trade exhibitions and export trade has increased. Women are, however, still absent in the decision-making levels. The United Nations Industrial Organisation (UNIDO) has been a reliable partner in marketing but its area of operations is very small and insignificant.

Technology transfer Women would benefit from improved technology to make the production process less onerous and the final output is more qualitative. Acquisition of technology has however been hampered by lack of transfer mechanisms. There are a few non-profit agencies which are promoting the use of improvised technology. The few initiatives that target women have shown that women are keen participants in technological innovations and are gaining momentum.

Research and development There are few cases of deliberate research and development programmes. The isolated cases are limited to the housing sector and quality improvement of a few selected items. Attempts to quantify women's unpaid work has been minimal. The character of R and D initiatives is slowly changing in line with economic realities and the spirit of gender sensitive development to encourage equity in policies and programmes.

Grassroots women have also made minimal inroads into the technological horizons in their endeavour for labour saving. The discovery of fireless cookers (to cope with energy crises) and charcoal coolers (to solve preservation needs) are more examples of their successes.

Recommendations

There is a critical need to promote economic literacy at all levels, regional, national, and grassroots. To initiate this education process the following could provide an entry point.

- More consultation should be organised between African proponents of economic empowerment and sister organisations in the North to demystify economic issues and encourage increased women's participation in existing economic blocks, trade agreements and economic support programmes such as the Structural Adjustment and Gender in Africa (SAGA).
- Pilot projects should be initiated and supported to encourage women to enter the mainstream of economic structures and programmes alluded to above.
- At the national level governments, NGOs and development agencies should take up the challenge of economic education and literacy. Specific programmes should be made part of the SPA package.
- Develop and disseminate genderised and tailor-made economic models that are appropriate for Africa and that promote gender equity. As a starting point officers of the World Bank and African development agencies should be introduced to gender sensitive planning and programming.
- Develop strategies for strengthening linkages between micro-level programmes with macro-level programmes and initiatives.
- Increase training and technical extension services to micro-entrepreneurs and smallholder farmers.
- Women, as the main food producers and patrons of local market centres, should be supported by local governments and their contribution to the tax base be quantified.
- Governments should be lobbied to pass laws that encourage equitable distribution of assets and income arising from employment and inheritance.
- Women's organisations concerned with economic issues should lobby governments and donors to promote human-centred development and initiate alternative frameworks to monitor development programmes.

Conclusion

While the status of women at the grassroots is still characterised by struggle for survival, their innovative strategies to overcome poverty are commendable. Women have said that the road out of poverty is difficult, but with adequate consultation and appropriate support the quality of life could be improved.

Note

1   These included: the Women In Development (WID) units in Nyeri, Vihiga and Webuye Municipal Councils; the President of the Council for the Economic Empowerment of Women in Africa, Mrs Beth Mugo; the Chairman of the Federation of Grassroots Women's Association of Kenya, Mrs Jane Kiano; the networking contract persons in Nairobi, Ms Lydia Kinyua and Mrs Elizabeth Njenga; the authors whose submissions comprise this report – Ms Betty Katarega Kibuka, Uganda/Mr S. Johanes Sebu Gawa, Namibia/Mrs Haile Yamatoworke, Ethiopia/Mr Ngaruiya Chutha, Kenya/Ms Jacinta Makokha, Kenya/ Mr Waruinge Muhindi, Kenya; Mrs Miriam Nguno of the Women's Bureau; Mr John Waithaka of the Ministry of Planning and National Development; Ms Shua Anyamba of the Kenya Management Programme. Special thanks go to Ms Margaret Grieco, World Bank, Africa region, Voices from African Women initiative for the financial support and D.M. Munge for his editorial services. It is my sincere hope that this collaboration is the beginning of a lasting relationship in support of women's initiatives to overcome poverty.

Appendix 1 Country Report: Uganda

Women's Initiatives to Overcome Poverty in Uganda

Poverty is a chronic phenomenon in most countries, caused by economic, political, social and cultural factors, many of which are directly related to current economic crises and the adjustment measures taken to combat them. Uganda is classified as one of the poorest countries in the world with a GDP per capita of $159. Uganda's poverty line is drawn at $100 a year per capita; this includes 55 per cent of Ugandans. About 57 per cent of the rural population lives below the poverty line, while the percentage is 38 urban population.

Poor households tend to be larger, have older household heads, and are more likely to be headed by a woman. At least 30 per cent of households in different areas of the country are headed by a woman whereas only 27 per cent of the women have a right to decide on the use of the income they generate.

In Uganda, like most of Africa, women have made significant contributions to the growth of the economy and social welfare of the people. Since independence, the rural women have been involved in the production of food crops. The surplus, if any, is sold to earn some limited income. This income more often than not goes to the provision of household goods and essential services like medi-care. Traditionally, women took charge of all domestic work which included household cooking, care of the children, elderly and the sick with little assistance from their husbands or male relatives.

Economic Activities

Rural Women

In an attempt to overcome poverty and improve their welfare, women in most areas of Uganda have set up income-generating projects and are thus engaged in various activities. Income-generating activity can be defined as 'any self supporting project where benefits accrue to women participants from the sale of items for money, from employment for wages or increased produce'. This encompasses projects which increase income through food for work projects, but excludes those which require continuous support and subsidy from outside. Such income-generating activities include sale of labour, surplus food, petty trade, informal savings and credit and even barter trade. Despite the constraints faced, these activities appear to be beneficial to rural women.

Urban Poor

In the urban areas, women are engaged in market vending (some sell cooked food, second-hand clothes), retail shops, local brewing, street vending (sweets, newspapers) and zero grazing. Digging for others (labour selling) and the supply of cheap garments and snacks to low income workforce are typically a women's informal sector job.

The Informal Sector

Due to unemployment or very low paid formal sector employment, an increasing number of women in urban areas of Uganda have turned to self employment in the informal sector. The major problem for these women is lack of capital.

Women in Micro and Small Enterprises

There are some women who have moved a step forward and are now medium scale businesswomen. Such women import merchandises like shoes, cosmetics, domestic and children's wear, hardware, etc. These women are engaged in trade between London, Dubai, China, Taiwan, Italy, Brussels, etc. Other women with little capital buy goods from these women importers and sell them on a small scale (retail) in the shops and even in offices. You can find about 15 women each selling their own merchandise in one shop.

The level of women's productivity or the type of income-generating undertaken is still limited by a number of constraints all mainly associated with access to productive resources.

Grassroots Women

In Uganda, women account for 55 per cent of the population, estimated at 17 million people, 89 per cent of whom live in rural areas. Although 97 per cent of the women have access to land, only eight per cent have leaseholds, and only eight per cent own the land they till. It is estimated that women in Uganda produce 60–80 per cent of the food for household consumption and also account for 70 per cent of the country's GDP yet all they produce is done on their husband's or male relatives' land. Despite this contribution by women, both in food and cash crop production women have not benefited. A major assumption in the recent past is that women will somehow benefit from the development initiatives simply because they belong to the beneficiary households. Programmes that seek to improve the conditions of the farmer have often not benefited rural women. Credit has always been accessed to the heads of households who are the owners of land without considering the actual person who does the work on the farm.

Women's Organisations

Like in other African countries, women in Uganda have developed informal grassroots organisations to support one another economically and socially. They carry out economic activities jointly and participate in home improvement schemes. Women also get to know one another thus creating unity of purpose.

Women in Uganda play a key role in development as they are the dominant producers processors and marketers of food. In addition to farming and home maintenance, they also operate petty business. They also participate in community, social and project activities.

Although rural poor women depend on the subsistence sector to produce food for their households' consumption, they have come to realise that subsistence alone is not enough for their livelihood. These women need incomes to purchase some of the monetised household goods and services. In an endeavour to meet this need, they have involved themselves in some strategic income-earning activities to be able to minimise the poverty.

Grassroots Women's Initiatives to Access Credit to the Poor

Finance is one major accelerating factor to development. Credit provides an appropriate means of raising funds for various socioeconomic development activities. Credit can be used for a variety of purposes – including education of children and for many other household needs. There is a growing recognition that institutional credit plays an important role in the socioeconomic development of any society. As socioeconomic development occurs, income rises as employment is created and entrepreneurial activities are intensified. According to the International Center for Research on Women 1994 credit is part of the larger picture of accesses to resources. Credit provides ways of assuring or enhancing women's economic activities.

A number of credit schemes have been established in Uganda, through the traditional banking systems and those outside. Although there are many formal credit schemes that target women, most women still do not have access to credit and therefore operate with a very low resource base. Some women have organised themselves in informal groups that raise and lend money among members. There is little on record about such groups, their experiences and constraints. There is therefore need to study women's informal lending groups, to help improve their credit arrangements and also open them to formal credit opportunities. Little attention has been paid to the existing informal schemes.

In Uganda as in other African countries, traditional savings and credit schemes exist and normally take the form of rotative savings and credit (ROSCA) which is contributed by members regularly and then lent to the contributors in turns. Women actively participate in this activity due to its simplicity and accessibility but the problem with such a scheme is that the amount which the women can save is very low. Due to limited sources of income and lack of opportunities to borrow more from banks, they cannot cater for meaningful income-generating activities.

For most of the poor, including women, who incidentally form the bulk of agricultural producers, borrowing seems to be the most economical form of exchange. This exchange is based on the use of kin and neighbourhood networks to borrow money that they can use. Borrowing is common in most regions of Uganda. Payment is usually in the form of labour and commodity exchange plus the return of the cash given to the borrower. Normally no interest is charged.

Women in Uganda are actively using various types of credit, e.g., Chilemba. Informal credit programmes range from one-to-one personal arrangement to group-oriented understanding on giving out loans. Below are some of the informal sources through which credit is given.

- *Revolving credit*: a revolving loan fund is developed with finances that come from within a group. The funds revolve from one person to another. Funds are made available for borrowing when repayment is made. For it to be operational, it takes good will, trust and confidence of each member in maintaining the revolving fund.
- *Rotating credit*: it is developed with funds from regular contributions made by members. Funds received are given in whole or part to each contributor in ration. This programme also requires good will, trust and confidence of each member meeting their contributory obligation to keep the credit

programme functional. A good example is that of women working with Lake Katwe Salt Project.

- *Products on credit*: another informal credit programme that is catching on now is that of credit through access to merchandise. Personally arranged merchandising networks provide women with products they could otherwise not afford. These products are made on common understanding of terms of payment. Usually the owner of the merchandise gives them out at a cost expected to be paid back either in lump sum or in instalment.
- *Rotating labour credit*: in another informal type of credit programme, women form a group in which they extend their labour to a person who needs services, e.g., farming, harvesting, weeding, etc. When these women are paid they save their money together or jointly and they agree on what to buy each time they are paid. It can be mattresses, bedsheets, cups, plates, etc. This type of credit programme is very common in the western part of Uganda mainly among the Bakiga and Banyankole. Some groups just extend labour to each group member in turn especially during the peak periods like planting and harvesting. This usually occurs in areas where millet and sorghum are grown because such crops need intensive labour which the women cannot afford to pay for. Therefore, they form a group in order to help one another. This is common among Banyankole and Bakiga of western Uganda. Loan savings is another type of initiative by grassroots women to access credit to the poor. Under the scheme the members contribute an agreed amount of money to a common pool from which loans for individual emergency need or school fees are advanced. Repayment is made as agreed without interest.

Appendix 2 Country Report – Namibia

Introduction: Country Profile

Namibia has a population of 1.7 million people (1988 estimate) with a growth rate of 32 per cent. It has a per capita income of $1,188 and an adult literacy rate of nine per cent. Its external debt stood at $340 million as of December 1989. Namibia acquired independence from South Africa in the late 1980s and was until recently grappling with a civil war between the government and rebel UNITA forces of Jonas Savimbi. It has two distinct economic classes which have their origin in the historical development of the country. The rich white urban Namibians who live in the capital Windhoek in luxury and the rural based black population who live in abject poverty. While virtually every white Namibian has access to excellent education, health care and other amenities, the blacks do not. Black Namibians are not only in poor health and have less education but also own fewer assets and do not have access to productive employment.

Main Economic Activities

The main productive sector is mining and commercial agriculture which is dominated by the white population. Commercial agriculture is the main source of income for the rural population and is of little significance to the economy as it is purely for subsistence. Fishing has great potential for development but remains unexploited.

One of Namibia's main challenges is the need to address the historical inequalities which have prevented the black population from having equal access to productive assets and services and markets. It must also maintain economic growth through public investment and providing an enabling environment for private sector to develop especially in the rural areas. The other difficult challenge is the creation of employment opportunities for the unemployed as well as former soldiers of the struggle for independence.

Poverty Profile

There are no quick solutions to poverty alleviation, but raising productivity of women who are the main family producers and creation of employment especially for the youth are critical strategies. Encouragement for the efficient use of labour and investment in human capital of the poor is likely to result in successful attack on poverty. There is need for increased expenditure on basic health and education services and establishment of safety nets for those that fall under the vulnerable categories. Other strategies include infrastructure improvement to enable the small farmers to reach the market. The promotion of the urban poor's participation in economic activities through the increased access to land, credit and the market is critical to poverty reduction.

Women's Organisation Movement

In other countries, women's movements thrive and have been a catalyst for the economic advancement of the rural and urban poor. This phenomenon is not visible in Namibia and is said to be underdeveloped or undocumented. The government, church organisations and NGOs have recognised the significantly disadvantaged plight of women and have made women, especially the heads of households, the primary targets of credit skills training and social services. Women's organisations in other African countries have been regarded as efficient conduits to channel poverty alleviation support to the poor. Namibian women should be supported in identifying existing groups and development of new ones. The strong community bond of the African people is visible in communal farming by the rural population. This bond should be exploited in strengthening women's organisations in order to enable them to effectively address key community concerns in health, nutrition, education and housing. Women's inclusion in poverty reduction initiatives is critical to their success. The rural women and the urban poor should be targets of initiatives seeking to cushion vulnerable groups.

Credit

Currently there are no formal credit markets for communal areas. There is need to develop strategies to meet smallholder demand for credit, especially for women who do not have land to offer as collateral. Grassroots women's organisations have been used to access credit to the poor and Namibian women should be assisted to adapt and apply credit delivery models that have worked elsewhere in Africa.

Research and Extension Services

There is a critical need for farmer education and extension services in communal areas in order to improve productivity and increase investment in more profitable crops as well as increased veterinary services. Applied research in agriculture to identify constraints on growth of communal farming is urgent. Women forming the bulk of the labour on communal farms should be primary targets for both education and research initiatives as well as the agricultural services.

Financial Sector

In the emerging financial institutions the black community is largely absent. As strategies are put in place to transfer income from the rich to the poor through the financial system, women should be considered among the special groups to receive subsidised interest rates, credit programmes and specialised women's financial institutions.

Primary Health Care

As the government redirects health delivery services towards the primary health care and preventive health approach, women are critical players both in the traditional sense and in modern medicine. They should therefore primarily participate in the development of community-based health capability as health workers and operators in feeding programmes.

Education

The adult literacy rate is estimated at 60 per cent, of which women are the majority. Since women are responsible for much of the family maintenance they should be encouraged to participate in the formal and informal education programmes. Lessons from other African countries indicate that women learn better when education programmes are run specifically for women and grassroots women's organisations offer opportunities for training in agriculture, family health and income-generation.

Conclusion

The poverty challenges in Namibia call for strategies that encourage improvement between races and between the gender divide. While the alleviation might depend on the rate of economic growth, the wide subsidies and transfer schemes for cushioning vulnerable groups and households must be put in place. In a country where 40 per cent of the households are headed by women it is imperative that women be the primary target of all poverty alleviation strategies as participants and as a target group.

Appendix 3 Country Report – Kenya

Reaching the Grassroots: The Kenya National Networking Study

The main purpose of the national networking study was to consult grassroots women on the effects of the ongoing economic restructuring and reforms and how they are coping with these effects at the family and community levels. It also sought to document the efforts of women group networks to mobilise savings and advance credit to members. This report document summaries of information collated from national level institutions, grassroot women's organisations and collaborators who support the women group movement.

National level institutions were represented by the Women's Bureau of the Ministry of Culture and Social Services (WB/MCSS), the Office of the President, the Ministry of Planning and National Development (OVP/MPND), the Kenya Management Programme (KMAP), the Kenya Women's Finance Trust, Barclays Bank, and Maendeleo ya Wanawake (MYWO). Their headquarters set policies, package programmes and implementation strategies to be followed by branches at the grassroots. The efficacy of agencies in delivering support to grassroots women is conditioned by the activities of the headquarters.

At the grassroots, dialogue involved women groups, government departments, NGOs, individual women, entrepreneurs and other representatives of organisations. The report also documents the results of dialogue between the team, the partners in Nyeri Municipal Council, Vihiga Town Council and Nairobi City Council.

Economic Profile

Kenya is a typical African country which is primarily a rural country where 86 per cent of the population live. It is also a rapidly urbanising country through the rural urban migration phenomenon. Kenya has a population of about 28 million people, according to the 1989 census, with a growth rate of 3.5 per cent and an adult literacy rate of 45 per cent. The GNP stood at 270 in 1993 with a growth rate of 0.3 per cent.

Kenya is an agricultural country relying mostly on coffee and tea as the main crops and maize as the staple food. Tourism is also a major income earner compared to other resources such as marine, minerals and oils. It also has a wealthy manufacturing base although in recent years the government has focused on promoting export processing zones. The informal sector, commonly referred to as *Jua kali*, is a major economic sector.

The major challenges facing the country are poverty and unemployment. At least 10 million people are said to be living in poverty, while over two million people are unemployed. In the area, the official rate of unemployment is estimated at 25 per cent while unofficial sources estimate 45 per cent, especially in the urban areas.

Poverty Profile

Poverty in Kenya is characterised by low levels of income, high levels of corruption, poor social status, and poor quality of life resulting in poor nutrition, shelter, inadequate basic health and education services. The poorest of the poor in Kenya include pastoralists, small scale farmers, the landless, the unemployed and the slum dwellers.

Women's poverty is exacerbated by limited access to resources, cultural constraints and inequitable distribution of incomes. The majority of women do not own property and cannot inherit. They are overburdened by work both at home and in the community as well as the workplace. They are discriminated against by culture, traditional beliefs and practices.

Women in Kenya

The situation of women is still characterised by continuous struggle for survival with the majority living in absolute poverty unable to meet the most basic needs. By and large, the poor situation of women is a reflection of the poor economic performance of the country. Unfortunately, the heavy burden of poverty generally falls on women more than the men because they have less access to resources and have the primary maintenance.

Women are increasingly involved in agriculture, commerce and industry. Unfortunately, no research has been undertaken to confirm the increased rate of involvement. It is however clear that more and more women have entered the economic arena, possibly because the 'independence day girls' are now middle-aged with many having left formal employment. The well-to-do have entered the business and commercial farming sectors while the low income earners and unemployed have entered the *Jua kali* and informal sectors. The manufacturing sector has not been actively patronised by women and remains the preserve of men.

At policy formulation levels, women are absent both in the micro and macro levels. At the micro level, women are absent in cooperative leadership, *Jua kali* associations and DDCs. At the macro level women are absent in marketing boards, advisory boards, planning authorities and national and international delegations where most trading and economic agreements are negotiated.

The absence of clear national policy on gender involvement in economic development has also been a major constraint.

The Women Group Movement

The women group movement took root and was recognised at independence in the 1960s. They formed around the traditional practices of sharing work on a communal basis mainly to share farm work (planting, weeding, harvesting, etc.) and house construction (thatching, mudding).

Since most African communities lived in the rural areas, that is where the movement took root first before coming to towns. Groups were formed to solve social and economic problems as well as organising cultural activities such as weddings and circumcision ceremonies.

The movement has grown at a rapid pace which was accelerated by the Nairobi UN Conference on Women in 1985. The introduction of Structural Adjustment Programmes has also increased the tempo of group formation countrywide.

There are over 26,000 women groups with over a million members in Kenya registered by the MCSS. These groups are formed as a result of social mobilisation to address social and economic problems. They have been recognised as one of the most significant participants in poverty alleviation in urban and rural areas. 10 per cent of these are involved in informal savings and credit systems known as merry-go-rounds. Other key activities include agriculture and livestock by 62 per cent of the groups, sales and services 18 per cent of the groups, handicrafts 12.5 per cent and social welfare.

The overall performance of women group movement has been moderate. This is because despite the enormous energies and commitment that the members of the movement have applied, they face mitigating financial, organisational and policy constraints.

The government policy on women and gender issues in general is to promote equity in development. The policy commitment is not however matched with allocation of necessary resources. There are several government agencies, NGOs, donors and private sector establishments which support the movement.

Role in National Development

In Kenya the women group movement has striven and has provided a conduit for reaching grassroots committees with new ideas, programmes and even propaganda. There is a scramble in this country to use women groups for various purposes including attempts to cover political mileage. The government, NGOs and church organisations have also recognised the potential of women groups and have made inroads to reach them.

The government in its policy framework paper of 1996 has identified women groups as a channel for disseminating technical information and home messages to rural women.

Activities

The activities pursued by women/self-help groups reflect their social and economic conditions which undermine the essence of formation of the groups. Diverse activities are pursued by groups to varying degrees of intensity and sophistication. These may be placed into two categories:

- social activities which include; home improvement, payment of education, health and bereavement expenses; exchange of experiences; moral support; cultural advancement;
- economic activities which include: income-generating projects, savings and credit facilities, collective investments, housing development.

The activities pursued by groups have changed in response to the completion of the felt needs, emergence of new demands, changes in the level of technology and the coming into being of new arrangements. Many groups interviewed had advanced the activities they were pursuing three times beyond the initial entry activity.

Group Management

Most of the groups are managed through the committee system. The executive committee takes the proactive role in initiating decisions but the entire management committee is involved in decision-making to varying degrees.

The office of the District Development Officer (DSDO) exercises a supervisory role to ensure that order is maintained and conflicts are resolved as they arise.

Economic Activities

Women in Agriculture

Agriculture remains the single most important sector in Kenya's economy, Kenya's agricultural sector and food security position on the whole grew at a rapid rate in the first two decades, providing for all food requirements and substantial incomes especially to the small holder producer. In the latter decades, production performance in this sector no longer guarantees security.

The government has laid down broad policy objectives meant to enhance performance of the agricultural sector. Implementation of policies have however been constrained by inadequate implementation capacity and inappropriate instructional framework.

Most women, especially those in the rural areas, depend on agriculture for their livelihood. They do this through petty farming or labour contracting. The government and other development agencies recognise the predominant role played by women in agriculture but little support is accessed to the women. Even when the man has little to do with it other than making land available, the income accruing from the farm still goes to him. There has been some improvement in the land accessibility by women. Existing land laws allow access and inheritance of land by women but the practice is constrained by cultural values and practices. Those who can buy land are able to do so. Only under such circumstances do women have both access and control over land.

Women in Industry

During the first 10 years of independence there was an impressive growth in gross investment in the country which enabled the manufacturing sector to record growth rate of 10 per cent per annum. This developed to between four and six per cent in the '80s but dropped out below zero in the '90s. Some of the causes for decline in the sectors growth are poor economic management, shortage of foreign exchange and growing consumption. Inadequate support of local entrepreneurs both men and women and the increased control by the government have stunted the growth of local industrial base.

Women are not visible in the formal manufacturing sector but there is a big promotion of women in the *Jua kali* sector. Since 1985 more women have entered the industry. A few role models exist. The agricultural manufacturing and textile industries have quite a few successful women industrialists. Their contribution has not been quantified even in the 1994 economic survey. A few development agencies have introduced women-specific projects to promote women's participation in manufacturing. The most notable is the UNDP-UNIDO Women project which has trained women producers in Nairobi, Nyeri and Mombasa.

The government has introduced gender disaggregated information in policies and reports. This is just a start and efforts should be made to apply this approach to all policy documents and reports.

Policy such as sessional papers on small enterprise lack an active plan and clear modalities of effecting the recommendations for addressing gender inequalities.

Some glaring constraints that hinder progress of women in business include:

- insufficient funds and lack of borrowing capacities due to lack of required collateral by loaning institutions;
- inhibitive family roles which leave women with very little time to concentrate on business;
- negative cultural beliefs that restrain women from owning properties;
- lack of adequate training and appropriate technologies to improve their status on non-financial promotional programmes.

Women in the Financial Sector

The financial sector grew in leaps and bounds in the '70s and '80s. As of December 1992, the financial system has expanded to consist of the central bank, 31 commercial banks, 59 non-bank financial institutions, 38 insurance companies, six brokerage firms, 56 higher purchase companies, the post office, 10 development finance institutions, private pension plans and 2,000 savings and credit cooperative societies. In 1993, the credibility of some banks was called to question and by August of the same year, several banks were declared insolvent.

The existing financial market operates under the Nairobi Stock Exchange (NSE). The government on its part established the Capital Market Authority (CMA) to facilitate and promote development of active securities market in the country.

Women's participation in the investment and capital markets sector has not previously been identified as an area of concern and is by and large unresearched and undocumented. Very few women have ventured into micro investment and the financial market. Groups in Kenya demonstrate a minimum level of understanding of existing investment opportunities.

Women's participation in investment is hindered by lack of information, discriminatory tax laws, and lack of support by financial institutions. Cultural beliefs, values and practices do not allow women to acquire assets as security for funds. Women lack financial knowledge and understanding to manage funds and investment. This sector has therefore been portrayed as the men's domain. This scenario is slowly changing and a few women have ventured into the sector.

Savings Mobilisation and Credit

The majority of groups in Kenya are engaged in mobilisation of savings for investment. Very few efforts have been made to quantify the amount for savings mobilised by groups. The savings are used to advance loans to members who later repay it at agreed rates of interest. Group savings are also used to finance groups projects such as land buying or for income-generating activities. Groups have demonstrated a remarkable propensity to save. Savings depend on members' economic standing and range from K. Shs 10 a month to K. Shs 2,000 a month. Savings may also be maintained in assets which can be liquidated for cash should need arise or in a bank savings account. Some groups have formed investment clubs where all the contributions are deposited to earn interest or buy shares on the Nairobi Stock Exchange.

A lot of attention has been paid to women's access to credit. One of the offshoots of the 1975 Women's Conference is the Women's World Banking (WWB), a worldwide association for accessing credit to women. Here in Kenya, the Kenya Women Finance Trust, an affiliate of the WWB was formed. Other initiatives have been undertaken by the government, NGOs and mainstream banks. In spite of these initiatives, many women are still credit-shy and others do not know where to get credit. Several studies have been undertaken on women and credit in Kenya. The latest study by KCB on the availability and accessibility of credit to women in Kenya was launched on 6 July 1994.

Two banks, Barclays and KCB, have specific schemes for advancing credit to women. Several NGOs including PFP, KWFT, PIDE International Toronto, NCCK, World Vision, K-REP and others have also helped develop specific programmes for women. Different NGOs use different approaches but the most common is the Grameen Bank Model which uses cell approach to credit guarantee. The Savings and Credit Societies (SACCO) have generated a lot of credit for women. Most of these women who have left employment and retired into business were provided start up capital by SACCO Societies. This input has however not been quantified.

The government advocates equal access of credit by women by supporting agencies and programmes which address the constraints inhibiting women's access to credit. Ultimately, the government would prefer a situation where women operate in the financial market on the same terms as everybody else.

National Level Policy Intervention

Policy Framework

Through the Office of the Vice President and the Ministry of Planning and National Development, the government set development policies such as the structural adjustment programme and the policy framework programme. It is also through the OVP/MPND that the effects of policy initiatives to ameliorate the negative effects of the policies should be redressed. The WB/MCSS is especially charged with the mandate of gender and development including policy and programmes, registration of women groups, technical assistance and advocacy. Banks receive savings from the public and use the money to create credit for investments. Banks may loan the money directly to clients or use other specialised agencies such as KWFT to reach specific target groups. Such agencies may also raise loanable funds from other sources including donations. There are agencies such as KMAP which concentrate on extending technical assistance where a gap has been identified in the development which brings grassroots women associations together to gain the advantages of unity in purpose.

The overall performance of women group movements has been moderate. This is because despite the enormous energies and commitment that the members of the movement have applied, they face mitigating financial, organisational and policy constraints. The government policy on the women movement and the gender issue in general is to promote equity in development. This policy commitment is however not matched with allocation of necessary resources. There are several government agencies, NGOs, donors and private sector establishments which support the movement.

Access to Credit

The government advocates equal access of credit to women by supporting agencies and programmes which address the constraints inhibiting women's access to credit. Ultimately, it would prefer a situation where women operate in the financial market on the same terms with everybody else. The government, however, does not have a single formal programme or even explicit policy guidance to support access to credit by grassroots women. Even the recently published policy framework paper of 1996 is silent about increased access to credit by grassroots women and only assumes that women will benefit through the small and medium enterprises strategy.

Banks on the other hand receive a colossal amount of savings from the women movement. Though banks may claim that they treat women as all other clients, their requirements, procedures, bureaucracies and interest rates cuts out grassroots women who are so important in the banks' capacity to create credit. Banks are yet to be gender sensitised and, because they are aware of the raw deal they give to small savers, most banks are unwilling to gender disaggregate their credit operations.

This means that grassroots women have to resort to alternative credit which is either accessed by the non-governmental sector or the women movement itself. Most of the NGOs which are active in accessing credit have saver capacity problems which limit their ability to reach out to the entire movement. KWFT, for instance, is active in Kilifi, Kwale and partially in Nyeri districts. Its scale of operations in these districts is very small.

The above scenario creates an environment for the active participation of technical assistance agencies to assist women in accessing credit training, counselling, information dissemination and advocacy. Technical assistance agencies report remarkable improvement in the performance of women enterprises once credit has been injected. The giant MYWO has not developed a credit access agenda.

Structural Adjustment Programmes

After failing to involve vulnerable groups in the process of formulating structural adjustment programmes (SAPs) and faced with the sobering evidence of apparent poverty, the government prepared a policy on the social dimensions of development (SDD) to address the plight of the poor whose ranks were increasing rapidly. The SDD programmes are at the packaging stage and will be implemented under the district focus for Rural Development strategy. Donor agencies, NGOs, and political parties are some of the other collaborators. The MCSS is not aware of the existence of the policy framework paper.

Technical assistance agencies have developed appropriate training modules to prepare people who are being retrenched or are graduating from formal training institutions to fit better in a SAPs environment.

Training

The WB/MCSS collaborates with other arms of the government such as the Ministries of Agriculture, Education, Health and Local Government to extend training to grassroots women on various development issues. The delivery mechanism is determined by the nature of training. Gender sensitisation programmes have been enhanced since the Beijing Conference on Women. The training function for grassroots women is basically undertaken by NGOs. It includes self-administration, awareness creation, entrepreneurship development, credit management, health and nutrition, adult education, etc.

Technical Assistance

The WB/MCSS extended assistance to grassroots women through district social development offices and social welfare offices of local authorities provide similar support. Technical assistance may involve follow-up visits, advisory, conflict resolution, transfer of skills, counselling and research and development. TA is a very important component of any other intervention.

Access to Economic Resources

It is the desire of the NGO sector that women be encouraged to own individual property and manage economic enterprises. This position is similar to that held by the WB/MCSS which is contributing to the task force reviewing all laws affecting women. Elsewhere WB/MCSS in collaboration with the Kenya

External Trade Authority (KETA) is also assisting grassroots women to expand export markets.

Initiatives in Nyeri

The field exercise was initiated in Nyeri Municipal Council which also served as the test base for the questionnaire. Nyeri municipality is known for its intense women groups activities.

In the following analysis, the general situation with regard to the respondents is summarised and then the emerging trends in accessing/extending financial assistance, responding to the effects of structural programmes and administration of soft wave assistance are examined in detail. As far as possible the issue of inquiries are examined together as reported from different perspectives.

General Situation

Grassroots women in Nyeri have organised themselves in women and self help groups as a strategy for overcoming poverty at personal and family levels. The effort, though driven by group members themselves, has been complemented by a host of community based, non-governmental, private, quasi-public and public agencies.

There are currently 1,495 women and self help groups in Nyeri district registered by the District Development Office of which 300 are found within the Nyeri municipal council area. The majority of the groups were formed in the last 10 years the period following the convention of the third UN World Conference on Women in Nairobi. Groups have on average 25 members, rules and postal address. Those groups which were interviewed had advanced the activities they were pursuing three times beyond the initial/entry activity.

Group Management

Most of the groups are managed through the committee system. The management committee takes the proactive role in initiating decisions but the entire management is involved in decision-making to varying degrees. Members are aware of their rights within the groups and, whereas most positions in the management structures are filled by consensus, the rights of members are respected and prevail.

The office of the District Development Officer (DSDO) exercises a supervisory role to ensure that order is maintained and conflicts are resolved as they arise. The municipal council has made available a medium cadre of officers who extend technical assistance to the groups in all areas for common interface. In all attempts to coordinate the efforts of all the actors who are actively supporting group activities and therefore, maximise effectiveness, a Women in Development (WID) committee was established in 1991 with the assistance of the Friedreich Ebert Foundation. The committee has been very active.

Savings Mobilisation

The majority of groups in Nyeri are engaged in mobilising savings for eventual investment. All the groups which were interviewed were mobilising savings through direct membership contributions, retailed earnings from group activities or soliciting the support of other agencies. The savings are then loaned to members who utilise the money for individual activity and later repay it at agreed rates of interest. The most common system of credit arrangement is one where the savings is loaned out in turn to members. It is called the revolving loan programme or even more fondly, the 'merry-go-round'. Groups have demonstrated a remarkable propensity to save. With an average annual savings of K.Shs 250,000, most groups maintain at least one bank savings account with healthy balances. Savings may also be maintained in assets which can be liquidated for cash should need arise.

Investment

Groups in Nyeri demonstrate a very appreciable level of understanding of existing investment opportunities. Most of the groups have advanced beyond the welfare primary production axis and are now engaged in economically more lucrative operations. Housing development, export trade, leather and textile production, horticulture and participation in the capital market are some of the activities that groups are engaged in. In fact all the groups which were interviewed had procured shares from the Kenya Airways primary issue and were positioning themselves for the next flotation. The groups are also ready and willing to learn of other existing portfolios and they are especially keen to know about the operations of the secondary stock market and the securities markets.

Internal Credit Mobilisation

Most groups advance credit which is generated from members' savings or development finance agencies to members project on laid terms and conditions. The amounts involved range from K. Shs 5,000 with a monthly interest of one per cent. Certain requirements have been put in place to safeguard groups from default, including vigorous vetting procedures, examination of character of the applying member, informal security and legal action. Repayment is on average above 80 per cent for group mobilised credit.

Group members also access credit for social activities, including payment of school fees, medical bills, offsetting funeral expenses and hosting wedding ceremonies. Social credits are normally advanced on concessionary terms and some groups would consider giving grants depending on the nature of the social problem. Group credit is so far the most dependable source of credit existing today. It is, however, severely inadequate as it addresses less than 10 per cent of members' credit needs.

Credit Programmes

A number of institutions have established branch offices in Nyeri for the purpose of extending credit to women and self help groups. The institutions represented include: Partnership for Productivity (PFP), Women Entrepreneurs for Industrial Growth (WEFIG), Kenya Women Finance Trust (KWFT), Kenya Rural Enterprises Programme (K-REP), Juhudi Project, Kenya Industrial Estate (KIE), the National Christian Churches of Kenya (NCCK) and Women Enterprises Development Initiative (WEDI). The government of Kenya once initiated the rural enterprises programme which benefited some groups.

Though most of the credit institutions are not restricted in their areas of lending, there are some which are sector specific. WEFIG, for instance, lends only material loans to women in leather works production. The lending policies are formulated in their respective head offices. The policies, however, benefit from the inputs from the operational level; branch offices are also allowed flexibility to adapt to local conditions.

In the majority of cases, credit institutions operate along the on-lending line. Groups are organised to receive credit lump sum which they on-lend to their members or use for group activities. In such arrangements, members guarantee one another and their group. The credit is largely self administered with the credit institution extending technical assistance.

Interest rates are, on average, reflective of the money market situation through with a couple of percentage points variance either way. Repayment to the credit institution is remarkably high – 100 per cent in the majority of cases. This is because groups underwrite for those members who default and then institute in-house recovery programmes.

Credit from this source is normally complemented by software provisions of training, extension service and technological advances. In the case of WEFIG, the package also includes identification of local and international markets.

Credit from Banks and Financial Institutions

Attempts were made to interview banks and financial institutions which have branches in Nyeri. None of those institutions which were approached obliged. It was, however, apparent from interviewing the groups that none of them had approached banks and financial institutions for credit. Even established women entrepreneurs had not commonly utilised the banking facilities. Indeed, those national banks which claim to be having special windows for women and the informal sector do not seem to have had an impact at the grassroots.

If one considers that the groups have maintained savings accounts with banks which have healthy balances, a parasitic relationship was established in favour of the banks.

Responding to Structural Adjustment Programmes

The effect of the World Bank/International Monetary Fund (IMF) driven structural adjustment programmes (SAPs) have been felt by the women grassroots movement in the Nyeri region. Women, as individual entrepreneurs and in groups, have found themselves on the receiving end of SAPs though they were never involved in the formulation and implementation of the programmes. To many, life has become increasingly miserable. All the welfare indicators have gone down and the situation would have been worse had the women themselves not come up with measures to counter those effects.

The policy objective of the SAP is not well articulated at the grassroots level. Even the government departments which are critical of expanding the policy demonstrated scanty understanding of it. The active players have had to deal with effects. Non-governmental organisations in pursuit of the SAPs have significantly reduced their commitments in the name of stability. The municipal council's social department has taken a more programmatic role of training women on how to cope with the negative effects of SAPs while at the same time taking advantage of the opportunities availed by the programme.

The respondents were mainly female adults with, on average, six dependents each. There are several household heads within the groups. Women in Nyeri understand the following policies:

- liberalisation of the financial market i.e. the liberalisation of foreign exchange regimes, introduction of *bureaux de change*, freeing of interest rates and capital market operations;
- cost sharing in health and education;
- privatisation of parastatals;
- withdrawal of food subsidies;
- participation in international trade.

The immediate impact of SAPs on women was unprecedented rapid inflation which set the prices of commodities rising beyond everybody's expectations. The cost of agricultural inputs and implements increased tremendously. This tended to affect domestic production negatively. At the same time, the food market was utilised which led to stiff competition from imports. Women were adversely affected because they are the majority food producers. The quality of food and food security was nevertheless not significantly affected.

Government introduction of cost sharing in health and education has greatly tested the ability of the majority to afford these services. Many private health services have been established and school drop-out rates increased. SAPs have also been blamed for the proliferation of squatter settlements and the widespread use of second-hand clothes (*mitumba*). The high interest rates on borrowing following the liberalisation of the money market has been a drawback on investments. On a more positive note, women have been able to buy shares in government-owned companies and those who are able can easily participate in international trade.

Six years after the SAPs were introduced, the majority of the women have found ways and means of adapting such that they can not be said to be any less powerful than before. This they have done by putting more effort in what they were already doing, devising new technologies and changing to new activities which are economically more productive.

Women groups have once again become the focal points for addressing the effects of SAPs. Emphasis has shifted to income-generating projects for groups and individual members. Nearly all women groups are operating a credit scheme based on the Grameen's model to boost capital formation for their members. The choice of investment opportunities has also become important with more groups and members opting for upper market portfolios such as leather manufacturing, horticulture and export trade. Activities are carefully scrutinised for their economic viability. Women groups have not, however, sacrificed the enormous social responsibilities befalling the majority of their members. Cash supports and concessionary credit is given to members who fall into hard times.

There are no public, private or quasi-public agencies which are deliberately addressing the effects of SAPs on women. Some agencies may be having an impact while discharging their traditional role of providing credit, training, technical support and research and development. Support agencies are, however, constrained by lack of resources and the absence of supportive policy framework. Most of the agencies, for instance, do not have development guidelines to implement the Global Platform for Action as formulated during the fourth UN Conference on Women held in Beijing, China in August 1995. None of the agencies and women groups had read the recently released the national economic blueprint styled 'Policy Framework Paper'.

Training

The majority of women entrepreneurs and women groups have received some form of training in specific activities such as: organisational and management of businesses and group affairs; self administration, project development and management; marketing, business planning and record keeping. Other forms of training have been general and include family planning, primary health, community management and adult education.

At the forefront of dispensing training is the Women in Development (WID) programme. Local NGOs have also extended training as a component of their programmes. The office of the District Social Development Officer is also crucial in providing training. The consensus is that training has had a very positive general and specific impact.

Technical Assistance

The women grassroots movement has benefited from extension services extended by officers of Nyeri Municipal Council and other department agencies. Specific problems and challenges are addressed. The services also include sessions to disseminate new ideas, advisory materials and conflict resolution.

Technology Transfer

Growth in technology has benefited many members at the grassroots with the movement from old technologies to new ones. The Friedreich Ebert Foundation, for instance, provided the aging women of Maendeleo with electric blockmaking machines to assist their quest for improved housing. Elsewhere, the use of sewing machines is widespread. There are support agencies such as the Kenya Industrial Estate which advance credit for improved machinery and equipment.

Access to Expanded Markets

Women groups have tried to expand their share of local, national and international markets. The Nyeri municipal council has been in the forefront. In providing women with display centres and ASK shows. Some women and women groups have even participated in exhibitions in South Africa with the support of the United Nations Industrial Development Organisation (UNIDO). Need has been identified for the formation of marketing cooperatives for women groups' produce.

Research and Development (R and D) and Other Activities

There were no reported cases of deliberate R and D reported in Nyeri. The Women Entrepreneurs for Industrial Growth (WEFIG) has, however, endeavoured to provide beneficiaries with up to date designs and product to measure to global competition. WEFIG is also conducting awareness seminars on gender issues.

Initiatives in Vihiga/Webuye

All the women groups interviewed are registered with the Ministry of Culture and Social Services. Their main reason for group formation is to access resources from the government, non-governmental organisations and extra partner organisation. They work together with the objectives of uplifting their families standards of living, improving the members' incomes and fighting poverty.

Activities

These range from the welfare activities of home improvement, moral support in times of trouble and contributions for health and bereavement expenses to socioeconomic activities such as 'merry-go-round' contributions for economic empowerment activities. The latter include agricultural equipment in horticulture and other farming activities to small enterprises such as eating places and tailoring enterprises.

Savings and Investments

The average annual savings range from K. Shs 10,000 to 30,000. Their savings records indicate that most groups have saved up to K. Shs 50,000 in the last five years. Over 50 per cent of the groups have benefited from the group mobilised credit and savings to the tune of up to K. Shs 20,000. They state that the amounts they are ready to borrow were as much as K. Shs 100,000. This indicates an awareness of the advantages of bigger borrowing. As well it shows the confidence the groups have gained from the smaller amounts borrowed, as their repayment records are generally good.

In terms of investments, the groups show an amazing ignorance in terms of shares and stocks investments and yet have ventured into the purchasing of plots and high grade cows.

Recommendations from the Women Groups

The groups recommended:

- soft loan schemes for women (one per cent interest per month): the government of Kenya should extend soft loans for women's enterprises as point of the affirmative action to redress the harm done by SAPs;
- lending institutions to waive collateral and use other forms of security. The grace period before repayment to be extended;
- that more women be exposed to investment education to enable them to utilise their savings optimally;
- that educational tours to other places be organised. (They indicate their willingness to pay for these.)

SAPs Position and Responses

99 per cent of the groups have membership aged between 30–60 years. Most of these women (60 per cent) have dependent husbands. The average number of children per family is eight and the number of dependents other than the nuclear family members is six per family. The top three needs that trouble families are school fees, health care and food sufficiency. Despite this position, 60 per cent of the respondents claim to that they have had to learn new coping skills by working harder, cutting down on unnecessary expenses and venturing into the area of small enterprises to supplement family incomes. They also attribute their success to inputs given by external agencies such as the NGOs, donors and local community-based organisations in areas such as training for skills development, technical advice and revolving loan schemes.

The group members have also woken up to their leadership potential and ability to influence policies at their levels by participating on local church committees, in the school committees and in the Maendeleo ya Wanawake Organisation leadership positions. 50 per cent have also participated in external shows and exhibitions and indicate that these have been useful in opening up their eyes to new possibilities.

Initiatives in Nairobi

This section of the report is based on research findings conducted in two slum settlements in Nairobi City. The research was carried out in Kangemi on the outskirts of Nairobi city and Mathare which is a slum settlement close to the central business district of Nairobi. The study was carried out by a research assistant with the help of a grassroots women leaders from the area. A total of 20 groups and 15 individual women entrepreneurs were interviewed. This gives a first hand impression of the urban poor in their own words of how poverty manifests itself and their initiative to cope with the effects.

Women are in the majority in the slums. They are single mothers and head of households in the forefront of most of the innovative community responses to urban crisis and community initiatives to urban social problems. They could achieve much more if genuine support were to be given by local and central government and other development agencies. Women groups which are community-based organisations have moved beyond the common support programmes to ones targeting all areas of development. They have expanded to such areas as environmental protection and income-generation.

Women in Slums

Due to reduced production capacity in the rural areas there is a growing flow of people from the rural areas to urban centres. The less educated, the landless, and the unskilled form the majority of these migrants. With nowhere to sleep and little or nothing to eat the disillusioned migrants end up in the informal settlements thus increasing the number of slum dwellers who eke their living from begging, hawking, illegal brewing, and other activities such as theft and prostitution. As part of the strategy to overcome the helpless situation they find themselves in, women have formed groups to address their social/ economic issues. Individually or in groups they start income-generating activities. They start by selling vegetables and other food stuffs or cooked food in construction sites. They are also involved in selling baskets, second-hand clothes and other household goods. A few sell food in kiosks. Those in production make handicrafts, building blocks and *chang'aa*, a local brew. There are others who end up as househelp, barmaids or shop assistants. The luckier ones might find work on the shop floor of a manufacturing company like those in food processing and clothes manufacture. Yet others start petty service businesses like hairdressers, *dhobis* (washing others' clothes at a fee). The unfortunate become 'commercial sex workers' which is the most risky alternative. The returns from all the micro, and illicit economic activities is very low and not enough to meet family and personal needs. Women are therefore forced to undertake several of those activities at any one time.

Cultural Disadvantages

One of the major contributing factors to the poor plight of women is cultural norms and practices. In most African cultures women do not inherit land and in some communities they cannot buy land even if they were able to. Income earned by married women is culturally considered to be part of the man's income and therefore under its use is under his control. Women have increasingly become aware of these cultural barriers and have attempted to address them both at the individual and group level. Land/plot buying is a common activity in groups that were interviewed.

Success Stories

In spite of educational, cultural and social status constraints, women in the slums – 'the poorest of the poor' – have recorded successes in overcoming poverty. Many have been able to support their families and dependents. Some have even been able to educate their children up to university level, while others have been able to construct permanent residential houses. Economically sound activities have grown to levels that are bankable and therefore they have been able to borrow from banks for business expansion. Yet others have started investing in quoted securities through a recent privatisation as strategy for building capital and collateral for acquiring loans.

Mathare: A Profile on the Area

Mathare slum settlement is the home of over half a million residents. Dwelling houses are mainly made of mud and old iron sheets. There is no drainage system in the area and sanitation facilities are nonexistent. Houses are haphazardly built without proper plans or access roads. Narrow meandering paths are the only access to most homes. Initially the government ignored the area completely. The communities therefore developed their own support mechanisms and as a result education, health, economic and even administrative structures are informal in nature. They were initiated by residents of the area. As an example most of the schools are informal and not linked to the formal education system. Even the first chief for the area was appointed by residents and was not recognised by the government. Initially all residents were squatters but some residents now own plots through the squatter upgrading programmes.

Profiles of the Women Groups

There are over 200 women groups in the Mathare area alone. These groups are both formal and informal. The formal ones, numbering over 140, are registered with the Ministry of Culture and Social Services through the local DSDO. The informal ones, estimated at 60, are not registered at all but operate on the same lines as the registered ones. They are run by committees headed by a chairperson with a secretary, treasurer and three to eight other committee members. Some have literate committee members but most do not. It is not usual for groups to have members of the executive (chair, secretary, and treasurer) who are completely literate.

Kangemi Area Profile

Kangemi is a location in Dagoretti constituency. Previously it was part of

Kikuyu District but due to the growth of the city it was annexed to Nairobi. Demand for housing precipitated mass land subdivisions into residential plots which were bought by people from outside the area. The new plot owners developed cheap housing some with temporary materials to meet the rising demand for houses by workers employed in government, industries and other enterprises in Nairobi city. The area was initially planned for low density farming community. Most of the new developments were constructed without due regard to planning requirements. Accessibility is however assured by the existence of dirt farm access roads.

Women Groups in Kangemi

Kangemi has a metropolitan community with most of the Kenya tribes resident there. The ethnic group of the previous land owners (Kikuyu) is still the majority in the area. The area boasts of 100 groups. Members of groups are more affluent than those in Mathare and run larger businesses. Most of the residents live in family owned houses. They also own building extensions for rent.

Single motherhood is a major problem in Kangemi as many unmarried mothers live there. The rate of youth unemployment is very high. The burden of maintaining grown educated unemployed youth is the most major constraint women identified. The informal sector in the area cannot absorb them and many have developed criminal tendencies.

Unlike Mathare where most businesses are unlicensed most of the businesses in Kangemi are licensed and are fairly formal with better returns.

Constraints and Successes in Nairobi

While groups in Mathare focus on members struggle to subsist against strong negative pressures, groups in Kangemi are better endowed and can afford to be more development focused. This is because most of the members own land or have rented permanent houses. The majority of the groups undertake activities related to house improvements or business. House improvements include making building blocks for construction of members houses or for sale. Some groups are involved in pottery or production of handicrafts. All groups have a social component to support house improvement (buying of utensils), payment of health or education bills and support of needy members especially single parents. A few groups are involved in land buying while the group runs a nursery school and a free nursery.

Constraints Groups in Mathare and Kangemi and by extension all groups in Nairobi are constrained by lack of resources, poverty and political interference. The critical resources lacking are finances, land and materials for production. Poverty has been on the increase, especially over the last five years with the effect of more children dropping out of school and going into the street, poorer nutrition and increase in child morbidity rate especially in Mathare.

Because of the levels of income members of groups struggle to meet basic needs. Groups are generally inward looking and hardly interact with national groups. They also are handicapped by the existing structure of women's organisations, most of which relate to grassroots groups only as recipients of support. The newly formed FEGWAK is working to address this need. Due to the above factors some of the groups interviewed were represented at the Beijing Conference. Two of the groups said they heard about it.

Achievements 1991–1995 In spite of the constraints facing groups in Nairobi some mileage has been covered. In Mathare the rate of children sickness has gone down due to improvements in sanitation. Many groups have bought plots or have identified donors who will finance the buying of land when found. Being a slum area from which they could be evicted at any time, this is a major achievement. Business are doing poorly but social activities have received a lot of support from development agencies such as Water Aid, churches and individual donors.

In Kangemi, members have constructed permanent houses through group support. Other groups have installed piped water and electricity.

Financial Profile of Groups

Groups in Nairobi have a diverse financial profiles and performance. Mathare groups contributions are meagre ranging from K. Shs 10.00 ($0.17) to K. Shs 100 ($1.7) per month, but are keen savers. The group with the least savings had K. Shs 20,000 ($360) while some groups had saved up to K. Shs 87,0000 ($1,600). Kangemi groups on the other hand contributed substantial amounts, ranging from K. Shs 200–1,000 a month but are poor savers with a total of K. Shs 20,000–50,000 ($360 and 900) respectively. One group had accumulated K. Shs 170,000. These low savings could be attributed to direct investment in materials for production and/or advanced to members.

Investments

Few groups are aware of the Nairobi Stock Exchange and the capital market and even fewer invest in securities. Most groups however invest in land. Groups indicated they would like to be exposed to the Nairobi stock exchange are part of a strategy for building capital that can be used as collateral.

Access to Credit

Groups mobilise credit on a merry-go-round basis where a group collects a pre-agreed amount from every member and advances to one or two members. The amount of credit depends on the group's monthly contribution and the number of beneficiaries. The repayment period is equal to the number of members in the group. There is no interest charged for this type of credit and groups are not to strict on how it is applied. Some groups however set objectives for each round and all members are required to realise the set objective. As an example the group might have home improvement as an objective of a given round whereby all members are required to use the credit to improve their homes. They could buy utensils, furniture or housekeeping tools and equipment. In another round, the group might make water conservation an objective through rain harvesting. Each member would use the credit to buy materials for water harvest, e.g., gutters, water tanks, etc. while members provide labour on a voluntary basis. For the Mathare groups most of the credit goes to family maintenance in the form of medicine, food and clothes. A small proportion goes to the buying of utensils as part of home improvement. It is estimated that groups in Mathare generate credit amounting to K. Shs 800,000 per year while Kangeri Groups save around three million per year.

Another type of credit programme is where each group sets a small fund, says K. Shs 2,000, for members to borrow for emergency. Some emergencies would be related to school fees, sickness in the family or outstanding bills like rent. Repayment is made the following month with interest set by members.

The third type of credit is the short term credit of up to 12 months. Under this scheme commonly referred to as the revolving loan funding, members save over a period to establish a fund from which members apply. It works the same way as the savings and credit concept of the cooperative movement and the money is paid back with interest of up to 30 per cent. Some groups receive support from NGOs such as KWFT and PFP on terms set by the lending organisation. The groups interviewed in Mathare do not operate either of these last two credit programmes, which are very popular in Central Kenya.

Recommendations

Groups expressed interest in the revolving fund credit programme and requested support in setting it up. They also requested a workshop on credit accessibility at subsidised rates of interest.

Poverty Alleviation Strategies

Most group members are heads of household in both Mathare and Kangemi, although female-headed households are more common in Kangemi than Mathare. However, 60 per cent of the married members of groups in Mathare live with a dependent husband. Most members fall into the 30–60 age category (40 per cent in Mathare). Only nine per cent of the members are under 30: Kangemi groups are aging with 20 per cent of the members being at least 60. Most members have an average of five children and eight dependents in both places.

As a result of poor economic conditions, women have been unable to meet their basic needs. These are adequate food for the family, education, health services, water and shelter. They have had to cut down on some or most of all these needs and concede that family status has got worse. Women have suggested solutions to these problems. They feel food prices should not be liberalised but subsidised, especially staple foods. They should also be assisted to get soft loans and technical support to small business. Being slum dwellers, resettlement would be the ultimate solution and should be given priority by the government.

Women are well aware of the policy and effects of cost sharing in health and educational and other SAP programmes. They are however not aware why these policies were imposed on them and would like them reversed. On the other hand, privatisation 'is for the rich' and does not concern them at all. They have to live with the resultant effects of SAP policies which affect them directly. There is greater demand on parents under cost sharing and members' contributions to groups have gone down as a result while businesses are experiencing low turnover.

Women Entrepreneurs

Women entrepreneurs were reluctant to give information for fear that the information would be used for tax purposes. Only a few responded and their input is summarised below. Businesswomen in Kangemi are advanced and have the basic infrastructure for business development. Many of them operate from owner or rented permanent business premises with water and electricity and telephone facilities. They also have post office boxes through which they receive mail. Most of the businesswomen are married and have basic education either primary or secondary level. None of those interviewed was illiterate. Most have supportive husbands and a few have dependent husbands. They have an average of five own children and six dependents (children inclusive) on average.

The main business occupations are trade and zero grazing of dairy cows. Some businesses started in the '80s while others are less than five years old. Most women started business as an alternative to employment and for income-generation. All businesses have expanded over the five years due to high demand and improved business management skills acquired through training by BIG through women groups.

Not all the women interviewed belong to economic associations such as the chamber of commerce, *Jua kali* federation, cooperative society or professional body. They have had membership of some but have not considered them critical to their business development. They however all participate in the agricultural shows which they consider to be educative. Business performance is much better than that of Mathare women. The lowest turnover recorded was K. Shs 10,000 while the highest is K. Shs 50,000 but this could be gross understatement given other performance indicators. Starting capital ranges from K. Shs. 4,000–10,000 provided either by women groups, merry-go-round or petty trading. Like the women in Mathare, most of the business surplus is spent on food for the household. This ranges from 2,000–6,000 per month.

Women entrepreneurs save between K. Shs 200–1,5000 a month. Some of this money is used as contribution for the group and the balance kept in a savings account. The highest women saver had K. Shs 30,000 in a bank account. Although all women were aware of the recent sale of shares for Kenya Airways, National Bank and National Industrial credit none had bought any of the shares.

All women indicated that they have been adversely affected by SAPs both at the household level and at the enterprise level. Some of the critical needs that have not been met are working capital, production inputs and markets at business level, food, medicine, school fees and employment for their children at the household level. The family status has become worse as a result of adverse economic performance of the last five years. This is mainly because family maintenance has gone up while enterprise incomes have come down. Most entrepreneurs have either supported their business in response to the changes or started other businesses which they thought to be more profitable.

Entrepreneurs highly appreciate the support they have received from groups where they are members. The merry-go-round has received special commendations and respondents felt that these initiatives should be supported. Few businesses received training and assistance directly but all of them have received support through their women groups by the Ministry of Agriculture and the BIG. They expressed a need for business counselling and more training in business management. Appreciation of the need for research and development and technology is very low among entrepreneurs. Production of building materials has been taught at group levels.

Request was made for increased transfer of appropriate and labour saving technology at family level these would release valuable time to be used in business marketing. Most entrepreneurs (five out of eight) appeared satisfied with their current market share. They however requested support to penetrate markets outside the country for groups' production.

Other constraints hampering businesswomen include duplication of business in that too many people were running the same kind business. Business capital is also diverted to school fees, health services and other business needs. As food prices go up, women become unable to pay even school fees and hospital bills due to poor business returns.

Women have responded to the poor economic conditions by joining for support, reducing consumption at home and consuming low quality foods. They have also had to reduce purchase of educational materials for their children. Some have started businesses to guarantee income while others have had to start selling illicit brews like *chang'aa* (Nubian gin) and *Busaa* to supplement their income. Those who now have to work longer to earn more to meet their increased needs.

Women in Mathare have not been completely forgotten. NGOs work in the areas to assist the communities. Key among the support received is customer and business management by Undugu Society, business training and loans by fault project, advice on project selection to meet customers needs as well as business training by Maendeleo ya Wanawake and the Catholic Mission. Most churches have also set feeding programmes for children in Mathare (soup kitchens).

On their part, women have tried to improve business performance by carrying out business assessment before setting up. Participating in the Mathare market days (Tuesdays), participating in a trade delegation to Tanzania and

Zanzibar has proved profitable. Asked to make recommendations for improvement they requested the sourcing of external markets for women's products and technological improvement for metal fabricators. They also requested for technical advice and design improvements of their products, increased loans for business expansion and training in business management.

Effect of Economic Policies

As a result of the liberalisation and cost sharing policies women believe that Mathare people are poorer. This has resulted in the increase of street children and beggars. The health of their children is affected due to poor nutrition and poor health services. Due to rising prices their purchasing power has gone down while expenditure commitment on basic needs has increased. Although a lot has been said about assisting the vulnerable groups, none of those interviewed have received any support relief, materials or otherwise. They have never heard of SAPs or safety nets.

Request for Government, Donor and NGO Support

Women would like the government to support them in the form of land allocation and loans to buy lands. They would appreciate TOL operation sites, materials on credit for construction of decent housing preferably on their own plots. They also asked for reduction of fees for health and education services as well as setting up of a welfare fund for the unemployed and allocation of land to the unemployed, especially in Mathare for slum dwellers, and better sanitation service by the City Council.

From NGOs and donor community women would like loans for business. They would also like capital injection for their merry-go-round through the revolving loan fund of NGOs like KWFT, technical support and training for business, lobbying for reduction in consumer prices and an increase in salaries of low income earners.

Constraints to Empowerment

One of the constraining factors to women empowerment is their absence from decision-making structure and processes. Asked what other activities they have participated in, they said that they participated in other groups, some said that they hold positions in Maendeleo ya Wanawake Organisation while others said they are traditional birth attendants.

Group Impact

All those who were interviewed said they have benefited from their group. Among group achievements are land buying for groups, credit to members for business and personal support during emergencies in the family. In the areas of training, technical assistance and technological transfer the group has received support. On support to other women in the community by the group, respondents confirmed that they supported neighbours with problems and gave advice to other women on matters of nutrition, family planning and child care.

Appendix 4 Impressions of a Mathare Resident

Background of Mathare Slum

Mathare was bush before Kenya became independent in 1963, but after independence people were free from colonial rule and they were able to organise individual ways of living. In 1964 a man from Ukambani called Mutisya built the first carton house and Mathere 1, which was named after him (Mutisya), was born. Mathare at present is divided in locations and villages, i.e. Mathare location, Huruma location, Kariobangi location, Karasani location and Githurai location. Mathare is located at the left hand side of Juja Road one and a half kilometres from city centre. There is a famous girls' school called Saint Teresa's. Mathare people use Juja Road from town. The road divided Mathare and Eastleigh Estates and on the sides of this estate then is a famous air base called 82 Moi Air Base, opposite Mathare. Mathare means 'to grab (*Guthura* or *Kunyakua*) what is remaining' so Mathare is in plural 'those who are ready to grab'.

Mathare is about 2,500 hectares approximately in size with a population of 200,000 people. The slum Mathare is densely populated and it is the biggest slum area in Kenya.

Groups' Reports

Wapenda Afya Bidii Women Group

It was started in 1993 as merry-go-round group. It had about 70 women at first and after staying together and sharing talks together they decided to have another activity of cleaning the environment when work started because people were not paid many refused to work. Those who were left are 38 in number and continued with both merry-go-round and cleaning.

In 1994 the group decided to be cleaning even the toilet No. 141 which had been blocked for a number of years to decrease diseases such as diarrhoea, vomiting, dysentery, Malaria and worms. Even now they are working very hard although they have a friend who sympathised with them and unblocked the sewer and cleaned the drains of waste.

The groups which is in Mathare 4B also has an office, water, kiosks and toilet charge as group income. The contact person is the Chairlady Gachii or

Secretary Doine Awiti.

The problems faced by Wapenda Afya is lack of technical knowledge and management. Tribal customs and taboos because the group is mixed by them also when working some of group members do not participate and they are best rumour mongers. Gumboots are also a problem.

Wamathina Women Group

The group was started in 1987 with ideas of uplifting their standard of living by working as a group because they were very poor at that time. They had tried their best to uplift their living because they had educated their children on Harambee basis.

They have managed to buy plots on their own and have started to build on harambee basis. Those women are very cooperative because even the day of the building they go all of them there. They are 30 in number and can be found in Mathare No. 3. The contact person is the chairlady, Wanjiku. The problem of this group is shortage of finance because those women had carried greatest burden of family. They are spending more than they can earn. They depend on small business and they develop the group. They sometimes use even the stock because profit cannot be sufficient to feed their families.

Mugambo Women Group

The group was started in 1993, they decided to form a group to help each other by contributing money to a fund. They then invest in charcoal and paraffin retail business. Their funds grew slowly and they were soon able to open a bank account. There are 30 members in the group and the group is located in Mathare No. 1. The contact person is the chairlady/secretary Ms Mbithe. The problem is only of money as their business is not doing well as of now. Their intention is to have a site to sell their wares because they are constantly chased by City Council and Administration Askaris.

Wamtoma Women Group

This group was formed in 1994 although the people who joined are not new to the groups, because they had been in other groups which are now dormant and have not been revived. The group was registered this year in March. They are keeping pigs, hens, ducks and cleaning the river banks and the environment. They opened a bank account and are contributing money willingly.

The group is registered with 70 members from Mathare A and B as are divided for simple management. The contact person is the chairlady Lydia Kinyua, the group is a collection of all needy and willing women because to work without pay is hard. The problem is only lack of sufficient money to promote rearing of pigs, and also a market to sell pigs to fetch a fair price. The pigs are kept in Mathare No. 11 and the office is in no 4B. The main idea is to buy plots for members to charge and develop our living houses.

Medical Health Clinics

People suffer a lot because hospitals are very expensive. Chemist for medicine to serve the Mathare community.

Business

To help women with funds to develop their small businesses to improve their way of life. Women should be empowered through their ability and interest to work together with hope and confidence to succeed. After talking with those women I understand that some have given up on life and are working for their last day especially the aged women.

The groups need to be sponsored and supported by people technically and financially, especially in times of community action so that better results are reached.

Appendix 5 Country report – Ethiopia

Women Initiatives to Overcome Poverty and Access Credit to the Poor

Ethiopia is a country with about 55 million people out of which 27.4 million are women, comprising 49 per cent. The (population) growth rate is 3.1 per cent which includes the country as one of the highest growth rate nations. 85 per cent of the population depends on agriculture which is so structured to impede productivity. There is also land tenure and land use insecurity and an underdeveloped informal sector.

Ethiopia's current socioeconomic situation challenges development: over 60 per cent of the population lives below the poverty line. Unemployment is rampant and environmental crisis is worse.

Ethiopian women are key actors in the development process, they represent 50 per cent of the workforce, contributing more than 70 per cent of the agricultural labour force. The rural women work 13–17 hours a day. Yet their problems abound. The total living of women is among poorest of the poor in the world. They are faced with high burdens of family responsibility, while at the same time heavy farm work in rural areas and overwork in cities have become their lot. Their role as water and firewood fetchers has also added to their burden. Yet their contribution remains unacknowledged.

Regardless of occupation, women are given second priority in employment and even in employment they are paid at the lower end of job scales. They are faced with problems of health and frequent childbirth, lack of education and very low enrolment for training. While they have a constitutional right to property, the level of awareness of this right is low. Their control over resources is highly influenced by tradition and they lack access to credit facilities due to the above diversified socioeconomic conditions. Women have been effectively disenfranchised from participating in the decision-making processes and resource allocation.

Anyhow, with all round challenges women face in the country, they have been struggling and are still struggling for the livelihood of the society as a whole, being the backbone of the country. As the country is recovering from a long civil war long lasting effects and launched new democratic system, encouraging women policy, women are much more involved in poverty alleviation, food security and environmental protection efforts. They strongly believe that the key to alleviate poverty is economic empowerment which requires access to resources and credit among many other things.

Women and Access to Credit

In order to ensure better access to food, clean water, health and nutrition, the poor, especially women, must become more productive through increased access to assets and more equitable income distribution. Women must be empowered to participate in economic structures and policies to improve their access to resources and especially credit. Above all one of the most important determining factors to empowerment is attitudinal change of women and of society as a whole.

The new democratic government in Ethiopia has given the opportunity to women to get organised. In this respect women's initiatives to organise themselves to tackle their problems in the area of skill development, access to resources, credit, etc., and insuring property rights to alleviate poverty are very significant.

Ethnic development associations of women like the Tigray Development Association, which is a role model in empowering women on the political and socioeconomic scale in both the rural and urban areas, Oromo Women Development Association and others are making encouraging efforts in the field in respective regions.

Religious women's organisations are also participating in their endeavours, there is also effort seen in accessing credit to the poor women in micro businesses, petty trade, and making and trade of handicrafts by the Ethiopian Women Entrepreneurs Association (EWEA).

NGOs are also seen to be doing their part in poverty alleviation by providing training, technical services and rendering credit to women as some of their schemes. Key among these are the Action-Aid Ethiopia, Africa Village Academy and Canadian Physicians for Aid Relief.

Unlike the past decades the attention given to women in access to credit trends are now positive. Though the amount of money women get is minimal to change their actual lives, there is strong hope to increase the women's access to credit. Demand is so high while the number of organisations experienced in credit delivery is low.

Grassroots Women Organisations

There are many women and other organisations making a lot of efforts to alleviate poverty and access credit to women. Most of these organisations are dealing with many socioeconomic development issues.

Women groups and formal business organisations abound both in the urban and rural areas of the country. They are engaged in income-generating activities to support their members. They advance credit to their members on a rotational basis for both social/family and business related needs.

The National Women's Association for Development (NWAD) is a grassroots organisation specialising in training, credit and technical services for women entrepreneurs. It is used in this report to describe grassroots women's association in Ethiopia. NWAD was initiated and established by nine Ethiopian women in 1992 who had observed the difficulties of women's access to bank loans. They started by mobilising financial and technical resources and it was later strengthened financially by a fund-raising programme they organised themselves. The efforts made by these women is professionally organised and carried.

Objectives of NWAD and Details of its Support Services

The objective of NWAD is to improve the socioeconomic status of poor women by giving them access to training, credit and technical services.

Training is provided to all eligible groups and individuals irrespective of the type of business or level of education.

- Gives training to participating women in the areas of small scale business management by introducing proper simple and practical business management practices including record keeping and marketing.
- Conducts training on proper utilisation of credits and obligations of loans as regards loan repayment.
- Helps them identify and projects manageable within their financial, material and manpower capacity.
- Arranges internship programme by contacting experienced business enterprises.
- Raises the awareness level of women so that they derive maximum advantages from the services provided from the government and non-governmental agencies at their reach.

Credit

- The association extends medium and /or short term loans for any production-oriented and service giving activity as well as any petty trade activities owned by women.

- The loan amount will normally cover 90 per cent of the project costs, however time limits can be extended in deserving cases. Nevertheless the maximum loan limit, be it to an individual or group, is $1,600 with a minimum of $8 (all $ figures are US dollars).
- The interest rate or service charge is lower than that of conventional financial institutions in the country.
- Medium term loans are repayable within a period not exceeding 24 months. Nevertheless the repayment period of loans will be fixed depending on the nature of the project, the investment and income generated. Short term loans are repayable within 12 months.
- Bonus is offered as early incentive for early repayment of loans.
- Flexible security/collateral system will be adopted including community reference, legal entity of cooperatives, groups and force savings accounts.

Individuals, women's groups and women organisations living both in urban and rural areas of the country and who are engaged or would like to engage in small income-generating activities can be beneficiaries or NWAD services. So far NWAD has trained 150 individuals and three grassroots associations have got loans. The amount advanced to individuals is between $30 and $80 and $1,450 to each association. The association requires a minimum guarantee. The guarantee can be given by anyone who is employed or have a licensed business however small. The repayment experience is good with a default rate of less than six per cent. The loan fund is financed by the Canadian International Development Agency (CIDA) and the operational expenses are covered by the contributions mobilised by the group.

Initiatives to Overcome Poverty

Enhancement of women's productive capacity to alleviate poverty is to be achieved through better access to productive resources. Removal of barriers that restrict women's access to economic resources is vital, including their access to credit. The above efforts of different organisations and women's associations should be accompanied by the government's continued support that would enable them to carry out their activities more effectively and with less difficulty.

- Credit to women should not only focus on petty trade and small amounts, rather to include better business ideas which require more money to promote

growth secure self-reliance and sustainable development by continuing effort.
- Financial institutions should create new procedures to reach poor women, using special guarantee mechanisms, easy access to information and training.
- NGOs should be able to assess the sustainability, profitability, and enterprise structure of their income-generating activities. Further focus on availing credit to the group and make it independent. The fund must also revolve.

It should also be emphasised that attitudinal change in women themselves towards credit and improving their skills is one of the important factors determining their success.

12 Problems Encountered in Promoting Women's Access to Microfinance in Ghana and West Africa

LORRAINE OSEI-MENSAH
GHANA CREDIT UNION ASSOCIATION AND COUNCIL FOR THE
ECONOMIC EMPOWERMENT OF WOMEN IN AFRICA

Introduction

First I would like to thank you for inviting me to participate in this all-important forum aimed at addressing gender and development issues in Africa. It is my pleasure to contribute a chapter and have the opportunity to highlight problems in the promotion of women's access to credit as a way of integrating women in development. This chapter has two main sections: the first section of the chapter reports on the experiences of the Ghana Credit Union Association; and the second reports on the first West African regional meeting of the Council for the Economic Empowerment of Women in Africa. Both sections indicate the distance still to be travelled in ensuring adequate access to microfinance for women in Africa.

The Policy and Action Plan of the Ghana Credit Union Association

The Ghana Cooperative Credit Union Association's policy and action plan for integration of women in its main operations has been a long term one. The objective of the policy is to ensure that women are accorded equal rights and opportunities in the process of savings mobilisation and granting of credit to promote provident as well as productive ventures. The policy also aims at affording women the right to participate in decision-making at all levels of the credit union movement in Ghana.

143

Our strategy is thus to work for change at three levels by :

- increasing the number of female membership and participation in the credit unions;
- formulating and promoting a gender policy based on this objective; and
- developing adequate programmes and projects that meet women's credit and training needs.

Our focus of activities is to support women in their roles as producers and workers in agriculture, livestock, fisheries, manufacturing, food processing and commercial activities. The noble mission of the Credit Union Association (CUA) led to the creation of a special window for women since 1988. This was a Revolving Loan Fund from which only women who either want to start small scale income activity or to expand an existing one could borrow money.

Setbacks and Problems

In spite of the existence of a laudable policy and the presence of the loan fund as well as the institution of a training package that accompanies the credit, many women have still not yet attained economic independence. A survey conducted by the Gender and Development Department in 1993 showed various reasons why women still lag behind.

The survey report pointed out that majority of the respondents (women) spent 80 per cent of their income on household expenses. This shows that even when husbands give the usual housekeeping money (chop money) the wife still has to top it up to be able to provide balanced diet for the family. We also discovered that many married couples lived in separate homes either due to polygamy or temporary separation in marriage or to the nature of the couple's occupation. Such non-co-resident marriages naturally lead to separation of male/female household economies, with the women living with the children and bearing the greater part of expenses on medical bills, education, feeding and clothing.

The survey also revealed the gradual increase of women household heads. 40 per cent of the respondents indicated that they were the breadwinners of their families either due to the death of their husbands or because the marriages had broken down. In a few cases, however, the husbands were still alive but had taken on new wives and shirked their responsibility towards the upkeep of their children. The phenomenon of women becoming household heads was also highlighted in the Ghana Status Report on Women prepared for the Beijing Conference by the National Council for Women and Development. It indicated an increase in average female-headed households from 29 per cent in 1984 to 35 per cent in 1995. It also stated that the percentage of female-headed households in the rural areas had increased from 40 per cent in 1984 to 47 per cent in 1994. Perhaps this situation might be one of the factors that makes formal banks disinterested in granting loans to women.

The prevalence of certain customs and traditional practices as well as stereotypes against women also contribute to women not seeking financial support for their income activities. For instance in the credit survey conducted by Osei-Mensah and others in 1993 some women stated that they feared to borrow in order not to bring debt to their husbands who might end up divorcing them.

In some Ghanaian communities, especially in the Northern regions, a women is not expected to control money. This stereotype led to some women borrowing only to give the money to their husbands or sons for safekeeping. Experience shows that in many cases the men either used the money in drinking or for other things without the wives' knowledge and the young men also migrated down south with the money to look for jobs, thus leaving the woman unable to repay the loan.

Again the lack of access to land sets a great hindrance to women who wish to go into commercial farming. In Hamile and other parts of the Upper West a woman mostly farms on her husband's piece of land allocated to him by his family head. Such a woman can therefore not seek credit to invest in a large scale agricultural venture where she has limited access to land and virtually no control over it.

Similarly in certain parts of the country women are not expected to rear or sell livestock. For instance in the Upper West and Upper East regions a woman is not expected to sell goats, pigs or fowls. Such taboos are serious constraints on the types of economic ventures that women can invest in and would therefore not be encouraged to seek credit.

The lack of ready markets and the absence of adequate infrastructural facilities for marketing of farm produce and other goods do not encourage microfinance to women. A visit to the central parts of Accra reveals the ordeal women have to go through to dispose of their farm produce. Due to the demolition of some major markets in the cities the women, both food producers and middlemen, find themselves selling on the pavements of major streets in the cities. They face a lot of harassment from city authorities. Such harassments no doubt have grave psychological consequences on the women traders. Apart from a lot of them developing hypertension, a lot more tend to associate economic success or prominence with social stigma and negative consequences. Such feelings result in some women resigning to their fate and holding themselves in low esteem. They do not want to approach formal banks for financial support partly due to their lack of access to other resources or that they fear to be stigmatised or even for the fact that they have lost confidence in the banks.

Report of the CEEWA Workshop on Microfinance and Gender in West Africa

Women bear a disproportionate share of the growing poverty in Africa. This has been the result of an uncertain global economic environment, persistent external debt problems and structural adjustment programmes as well as civil strife. The extra burden on women stems from the absence of economic opportunities and autonomy, land ownership and inheritance, education and support services and women's minimal participation in decision-making.

Women constitute over 51 per cent of Africa's population with 70 per cent living in rural areas. They are primary producers of food and contribute significantly to economic life everywhere and yet they are largely excluded from economic decision-making. More specifically, lack of access to credit constitutes a major constraint on the effective enhancement of women's productive roles in Africa.

In view of their tremendous contributions to the economy of Africa the issue of poverty alleviation among women featured prominently on the agenda of the NGO forum organised in Dakar, Senegal in November 1994 in preparation for the United Nations Fourth World Conference on Women in Beijing, China in 1995.

At the Dakar conference, the workshop on women's responses to economic policies in Africa recommended that a permanent council be set up to lobby for the adoption of the section on economic empowerment i.e. poverty alleviation among women, within the African Platform for Action and monitor its implementation as well as evaluate results. The Council for the Economic Empowerment of Women in Africa (CEEWA) was thus formed as an African non-governmental organisation whose overall mission was to champion the economic empowerment of women.

CEEWA therefore has branches in various African countries, which are mandated to put in place strong machineries to persuade their governments to live up to their promises made when ratifying the Beijing Conference declarations. Member countries were also to create fora for women to meet and discuss issues of economic concern and share ideas and to ensure that women's economic empowerment is at the forefront of policy formulation and implementation at the grassroot, national, regional and international levels.

Objectives of the Workshop and Workshop Methodology

It was with the above mandate that CEEWA-Ghana organised its first sensitisation and awareness creation workshop on 'Microfinance and gender in West Africa' on 16–17 May 1996 at the North Ridge Hotel in Accra. The workshop's objectives were to exchange information on factors that impede women's access to credit. Two main areas were addressed:

- exchange of information on formal and informal credit systems available to women in West Africa;
- strategies/mechanisms for women's empowerment.

The workshop brought together 34 people made up of representatives of non-governmental organisations (NGOs), formal and informal banking institutions, and a few individual women traders. In all, three countries of the West African sub-region were represented, namely Ghana, Nigeria and Senegal. Due to limitation of funds not many countries could be invited to participate. We are looking forward to more financial support to enable us to involve all countries of the sub-region in our future programmes. The opening ceremony was brief and was presided over by the Executive Director of Empretec, an institution which trains people in entrepreneurial skills, Mrs Felicity Amoah. The country coordinator and president of CEEWA, Mrs Lorraine Osei Mensah, gave a welcome address and outlined the objectives of CEEWA and the workshop. She expressed the hope that all NGOs, institutions and individuals present would collaborate and network on a continuous basis to influence government policies in order to improve the economic status of women. She said CEEWA-Ghana was working on a structure that would make it possible for all levels of women, especially the grassroots, to have a voice in economic decision-making at all levels of the country.

The workshop was officially opened by Mrs Gloria Nikoi, an economic consultant, who in her key note address welcomed the creation of CEEWA-Ghana which brings together women from various African countries to discuss and share experiences and thus strengthen their capacity for working together for change in mainstreaming women's concerns in national, regional and international development priorities and structures.

The opening ceremony was followed by the various country presentations and other topics by facilitators after which members broke into three syndicate groups for discussions on various topics bordering on the workshop objectives. The following is an overview of common features and experiences gathered from the presentations and group discussions.

- It became evident that lack of collateral, stringent loan requirements, time constraints, high illiteracy rates, at times limited technical skills and/or managerial capacities, high interest rates and limited market outlets are some common factors which impede women's access to micro-credit.
- Further, results from the group discussions showed that only those microfinance programmes which paid attention to women's specific conditions and credit needs were able to achieve a considerable percentage of female clients.
- Thus with respect to the above only local savings and credit schemes – credit unions, susu or tontines, often formed the basis for women's savings and credit needs.
- Most formal banks favoured lending to medium scale enterprises due to low risk factors, thereby leaving out the large segment of female small scale enterprise.
- Most lending programmes were based on commercial interest rates. Lending to women borrowers with loan approval based upon economic criteria accompanied with appropriate loan monitoring usually leads to high repayment rates.

Lastly, it was a general view that formal banking institutions should link up with informal savings and credit systems to facilitate micro lending as the latter has the expertise for managing small loans at less operational cost. Furthermore, governments need to put in place policies that promote poverty alleviation among women and see to the effective implementation and monitoring of such policies.

Summary of Group Work

The issues discussed were:

- How can women's groups influence government policy on credit and poverty reduction among women?
- What can women's groups do to support the National Council for Women and Development (NCWD) to enhance women's status?
- What skills do women need for their business?
- What changes can we suggest to formal and informal banks to improve women's access to credit?

Group one The following summarises the ideas and recommendations on how women's groups can influence government policies on poverty reduction.

- Women's groups and professionals should examine government's policy regulatory environment concerning poverty reduction and use advocacy as a means of addressing issues.
- Specialised banks should be made to per their assigned functions, e.g., the Agricultural Development Bank (ADB) must finance agricultural ventures with special schemes for rural agro-based activities. Similarly the Bank for Housing and Construction should grant mortgage loans.
- Government needs to give incentives to the banks to perform in the sectors they are specialised in by way of tax rebates.
- Government should motivate banks to support new inventions, manufacturing, research, etc.
- There is the need for strong linkages between formal and informal banks.

Group two The group discussed the kinds of skills training that women need in the light of the realisation of the need for changes in training content methodologies to enable women entrepreneurs meet current market demand.

- Technical/technological skills specifically addressing enterprise, e.g., food processing, weaving, soap making/garment production, fish processing, etc.
- Managerial and business skills – conducting simple market survey, preparing business plans, writing project proposals, keeping efficient business records, etc.
- Skills for entrepreneurial and non-traditional career diversification, e.g., creating innovative ventures, branching into jobs dominated by men and which offer higher income, etc.
- Information and skills for competing on the international market, i.e. producing goods for export.

- Skills for quality control.
- Training/information on alternative banking options and how to successfully negotiate credit or loans.
- Literacy classes to enable illiterates keep records on their businesses.

Group three The group set out to answer the question: What role can women NGOs play to support CEEWA and the National Council for Women and Development and to enhance the status of women? It made the following recommendations.

- To network and establish a strong support for all women, more specifically for those women in public life.
- Women groups should form watchdog committees on the enactment and implementation of government policies and also lobby people in authority to influence policy decisions that affect women.
- Women groups should lobby for the quota system as a stepping stone for women's emancipation and gender equity.
- There is a need to have an NGO umbrella body to coordinate all women's organisations.
- Women NGOs should establish data banks and disseminate information regarding credit opportunities, sources of raw materials and other resources, etc.
- Compile a directory on women achievers, e.g.,
  How many women are in parliament?
  How many women made over 10 million cedis net profit a year on their businesses?
  How many young women graduated from post-secondary school?
  How many women entrepreneurs employ more than five staff?
  How many women are household heads? and
  How many women are above the poverty line, etc.?
  This data will show how many women are not making it and where we need to direct our support.
- Women's groups should support the creation of the Afrika Women Bank and advocate for 60–70 per cent shares owned by women.
- Information and documentation centres should be created in all regions and women made aware of the usefulness of such centres.
- Women in the media should be involved in the dissemination of information and research findings for the enhancement of women.
- Mobile cinema vans, drama groups, seminars and workshops should be

available in both rural and urban areas for educating and sensitising women and men about issues that are of concern to women.
- Exchange programmes should be organised within the West African sub-region to facilitate exchange of ideas and information.

Workshop Recommendations

The workshop ended by recommending that:

- CEEWA activities be taken to the grassroots and involve as many women as possible;
- CEEWA activities be given extensive publicity through the radio, newspapers, television, banners, etc;
- regional and local level seminars be organised to enlighten women about government policies regarding poverty reduction and opportunities for microfinance;
- the structure of CEEWA be finalised as soon as possible to give way to grassroots involvement;
- CEEWA should endeavour to secure office accommodation;
- a seminar be organised in Accra to enable representatives of formal and informal banks to enlighten women about what facilities for microfinancing are available for them.

Conclusion

The foregoing discussions have major consequences for the ways in which gender in poverty reduction strategies should be measured, addressed and targeted within our economy. This implies that poverty-monitoring instruments which rely solely upon conventional household survey instruments and techniques cannot capture adequately the gender dimensions of poverty. The result of such surveys can also impact negatively on services designed and delivered if women are to benefit from such services.

Any gender framework for Ghana should therefore consider that Ghana is a society where polygamy, spousal separation, separate husband and wife income and expenditure are prevalent, all of which set high financial demands on women as they shoulder greater responsibility for their children. Women's reproductive roles therefore impact greatly on their productive roles. Consequently, women's economic activities are largely in the informal sector and of a petty character. For these reasons, women's earning capabilities should become a key strategy for gender improvement in our country.

In closing, it should be noted that the participants of the CEEWA workshop on microfinance were grateful to CEEWA-Ghana, the workshop organisers as well as the Voices from African Women for bringing them together to share ideas and experiences on a subject that is very vital to the economic empowerment of women. The opportunity to publish this chapter has enabled those ideas and experiences formed from the grassroots to reach beyond Ghana to a wider audience and hopefully to reach the attention of policy-makers and development professionals.

List of Participants at CEEWA Workshop on Microfinance

Dr Stella Williams, Box 4088, Oshodi, Lagos State, Nigeria.
Funsho Raji, Box 4088, Oshodi, Lagos State, Nigeria.
Celeste Krahene Williams, FIDA, Box 16502, Accra.
Mary Tweneboa-Kodua, GAW, Box 93521, Airport Accra.
Joana Bannerman, GBC/WIB/ASWIM, Box 1633, Accra.
Hannah Agyemang, GROOTS INT., Box 1572, Accra.
Regina Degadjor, Lolornyo Women's Club, c/o Box 1562, Accra.
Gifty Ohene-Konadu, NCWD, Ghana.
Lorraine Osei-Mensah, CEEWA, Ghana.
Theodora Nti-Appiah, Non-Formal Education Divisional Headquarters, PO Box M45, Accra.
Kofi Larweh, NFED, Daugme, East Ada.
Stella Nitori, Christian Mother Association, Tamale, North Ghana.
Regina Azantilon, Christian Mothers Association, PO Box 5, Bolgatanga.
Victoria C. Koomson, Central and Western Fishmonger Improvement Association, PO Box 98, Cape Coast.
Fadiop Gueye Sali, SOSECAF/ Senegal.
Rebecca Adotey (now a member of parliament), NCWD, PO Box M53, Accra.
Kate Abbam, ASAWA, PO Box 5737, Accra-North.
Matilda Randolph, ASAWA, PO Box 5737, Accra North.
Hannah Abban, ASAWA, PO Box 5737, Accra-North.
Mary Otoo, ASAWA, PO Box 5737, Accra-North.
Jane Kinful, CUA, PO Box 164, Cape Coast.
Sharon Pitt, CSHRDC/WILDAF, PO Box 9070, Airport Accra.
Doreen Alotey, *Times*.
Marilyn Awuah-Asamoah, *Times*.
Blay Gibbah, *Times*.
Mirjam Schaap, FAO, PO Box 1628, Accra.
Augustine Quashigah, GROOTS INT., PO Box 1562, Accra.
Frances M. Hagan, PLAN International, Private Mail Bag, Osu, Accra.
Mary Kpordotsi, C.M.A.

Felicity Acquah, Empretec Ghana Foundation, PMB, Ghana.
Gloria Nikoi, Economic Consultant, Accra.
Portia Teye-Agbek, Jamestown Compound, Prisons, Accra.
Christine Dadson, Ghana Savings and Loans, PO Box 353, Accra.
Stella, Private Eye.
Kofi B. Abyen, World Bank, Accra.
K. Appiah-Kubi, G.B.C. Programmes.
Charity Acquah, Ghana News Agency PO Box 2118, Accra.
Ama Kudom-Agyeman, GBC Radio News, Accra.
Fred Otoo, Graphic Corp., Accra.
Rosemary Ardeyfio, Graphic Corp., Accra.
Adolphine Agyir, G.E.S., Accra.
Yvonne Wallace-Bàrew, CEEWA.
Rosemary Williams, CEEWA.
Regina Richter-Eshun, Y.W.C.A., PO Box 1504, Accra.
Florence Bithaman, SEHUP, PO Box 36, Madina.

13 Filling the Policy Gaps in Women's Economic Empowerment in Africa

BETH MUGO
COUNCIL FOR THE ECONOMIC EMPOWERMENT OF WOMEN IN
AFRICA, KENYA

Introduction

The depressing performance of African economies is a much discussed subject. News from the continent tends to be a tale of woe: starvation, food insecurity, civil war, social strife, political stress, declining health and personal insecurity are some of the most frequent themes we hear about. Though that depressing picture is now being changed by signs of hope, the general prognosis remains grim. A look at the key indicators confirms that even with the new signs of hope a lot remains to be done. More than 30 per cent of Africa's population lives below the poverty line. The actual numbers are presently estimated between 250–300 million people, representing about 10 times the population of an average size country like Kenya. The annual growth rates have been on a decline. The average for the years 1980–1993 was 1.5 per cent. Population has however grown at the rate of 2.8 per annum. This means that in many economies growth has been negative. Infant and maternal mortality are still unacceptably high. The infant mortality rate for sub-Saharan Africa is about one and a half times more on average than for all developing countries.

Much of this data is easily available and is generally widely known. Indeed many of the policy measures currently being undertaken by various African governments are geared towards revamping the African economies and stemming the continued downward spiral of the economies.

I do not intend in this chapter to go over the same old arguments. Instead, I wish to offer my initial thoughts on what I see as lacking in current policy thinking on the question of poverty reduction and its relationship to women's economic empowerment. Since the mid-'80s and more clearly after the 1990s,

154

it has become widely recognised that the gender dimension of economic policy must be taken on board if lasting solutions to Africa's problems are to be found.

I do not wish to detain you here with a lengthy account. My intention is to put some flesh on some of the arguments that we have been making over the last 10 years or so. I begin by putting on the table some of the issues with which we in the Council for the Economic Empowerment of Women in Africa (CEEWA) are concerned. In particular, I wish to focus on three or so critical areas in which I think reform is both urgent and desirable. As I make clear towards the end of this chapter, enhancing the capacity of women's organisations is the key policy measure to empowerment. Women need to develop the skills they need in order to identify barriers to their progress. I shall have something to say about what and how donors and other support groups can do to help in this process.

My discussion is organised around three thematic areas: in the first section, I explore some familiar territory. In keeping with that wisdom I look at the gender context of existing economic policies, highlighting some of the ways in which policy impacts on women. In the second section, I then move on to some of the institutional mechanisms for reforming Africa's economies. I invite you to consider the limitations inherent in some of these institutions. Some of these institutions include the state, the donors and civil society organisations. I suggest that it is important for us to explore some of the actual ways in which such institutions may aggravate rather than eradicate poverty. In particular, I observe that there is a need to scrutinise carefully the role of donors – multilateral and bilateral – and the impact of their policies on women. In the final section, I move on to the practicalities of policy. What are some of the concrete things that could be done in order to facilitate the process of economic empowerment for women? How, in other words, can African countries create a woman-friendly environment? This part puts some recommendations and suggestions forward.

Economic Decay and its Impact on Women

It is said that one can prove anything with statistics. I am not that cynical. Statistics can and do tell an important story more dramatically if and when they are carefully used. We have already seen that the overall performance of the African economy hardly inspires hope. I wish to focus attention on the gender dimension of that depressing picture. I shall concentrate on only five broad areas: political power, food security, health, education and personal security. I shall ask you to excuse this narrow focus. There are many areas we could discuss but then we might be here for a long time.

Political Power

Reflecting the generally subordinate position of the African women the distribution of political power in sub-Saharan Africa is heavily weighted in favour of men. You may be puzzled that I am treating the question of political power under economic empowerment. This is deliberate. I believe strongly that the weak position occupied by women in economic life in Africa is essentially a reflection of their political powerlessness. Seek ye first the political kingdom, Kwame Nkurumah used to say, and other things shall be added unto you. So too for women.

Part of the problem is the fact that in Africa the state is essentially an instrument for rewarding supporters and punishing the disloyal. Access to political power can make the difference between life and death.

How well represented are women in the institutions of the state in Africa? As you probably expect, not well at all. Women hardly feature in crucial decision-making organs. Only 9.9 per cent of seats in parliament in sub-Saharan Africa are held by women. When we turn to administration and managers, only 10.2 per cent of these are women. Yet it is these administrators who implement policy. The statistics improve only a little when we consider professional and technical workers. In these categories, women comprise a low 27.9 per cent of all the numbers in position.

One need not speculate but it does appear that there is a strong correlation between the low status occupied by women in society and the roles they play in the political and administrative mainstream.

Women and Food Security

The picture of an unhealthy mother holding the hand of a child with a distended stomach has, to our eternal shame, become the symbol of Africa's incapacity to feed itself. The African Platform for Action puts the matter fairly dramatically. Since 1960 the population of Africa has grown at an annual rate of three per cent. How about the continent's capacity to feed the population? Food production has grown at an annual rate of about 1.8 per cent. This means that Africa now suffers a structural food deficit.

The consequences of this food deficit are clear. For a start, more and more Africans are food poor. In less technical language, this means that the average African is not able to consume 2,250 calories of food per day. The actual daily intake of calories is just over 2,000 calories. Secondly, the growing food insecurity has generated serious health problems which, in turn, have only served to undermine the capacity of the average adult to engage in productive labour.

When you consider the impact of this food insecurity on women and children, the picture is even gloomier. Women are Africa's food providers and managers. Over 35 per cent of households of rural Africa are female-headed. In some countries, where there are huge mining businesses the figures are even higher. In such economies more and more men leave the rural areas to seek semiskilled work in the mines.

Two things seem to me to be lacking in current food production policies in Africa. First, the incentives that the governments use in order to enhance food productivity are sometimes horribly biased against women. In Kenya, just to give an example, machinery that is used by large scale farmers – combine harvesters, milking machines and poultry incubators – is exempt from customs duty and value added tax. Handcarts, hoes and other small holder tools still pay exorbitant duties and value added tax.

When you consider the size of the small scale sector these policies are clearly irrational. There are just under three million small scale farmers in Kenya. A whole 30 per cent of households in rural Kenya are female-headed. In some areas, this figure is as high as 60 per cent. Clearly, this type of tax structure punishes the small scale farmer and penalises women much more.

Everywhere in Africa, credit policies are biased away from agriculture. In this, again the case of Kenya is probably typical. Agriculture receives only 10 per cent of the total lending in the economy. More dramatically, the small scale sector receives only two per cent of this 10 per cent. Even this two per cent is, however, biased towards cash crop production.

A third area of food policy reform that is still a major problem in Africa is women's access to and control of land. Land ownership is still a man's preserve. Its disposal and use is still determined to a large extent by what the menfolk say. Again, it is difficult to imagine food security without land reform. Moreover, the rapidly growing population has deepened the land crisis. The average size of landholding by the household has been falling as more and more people subdivide their pieces.

Clearly as the land question is tackled policies also need to address the question of technology transfers. What technologies are we going to use to enhance food production? Do women have the skills to use these technologies?

How can we assist them to become consumers and users of these technologies? What is the role of donors in this?

My point is simple. There can be no successful policies to revitalise agriculture that do not address the gender dimensions of food production.

Women and Health

Health remains a serious matter in Africa. Too many people still die from preventable illnesses such as dysentery and malaria. Millions of others waste away due to poor sanitation and unclean water. Infant and maternal mortality are still too high. 76 per cent of the countries with the highest infant mortality rates are in sub-Saharan Africa. The percentages are similar for maternal mortality. Only 44 per cent of Africa's population has access to clean water. The risk of maternal death for the African women is one in 20. For developed countries the figure is one in 10,000.

In specific countries, the statistics are even more depressing. My own country is a case in point. In 1993 alone, there were 167,000 births to girls aged between 15–19. This was the equivalent of 18 per cent of all births in the country. 50 per cent of all serious abortion-related problems among unmarried women were amongst schoolgirls. Though the figures vary from country to country, the health problems associated with these are too grave to be ignored. Cases of perforated uteruses, ectopic pregnancies and infertility are on the rise across the continent.

I take the position that no one can begin to address the question of women's empowerment without addressing their health.

Women and Education

The capacity of women to gain access to education and to effectively utilise existing educational institutions is still deeply undermined by a variety of culture and policy biases. In some countries education policies expressly prohibit school re-entry after a girl has got pregnant. More often than not, girls in such school systems are forced to make the painful choice between school and a child. This in practice translates itself into a choice for abortion. Given that in fact many countries may have in addition laws that prohibit abortion, the girl may then be driven into the hands of quacks and unscrupulous doctors. In Kenya, for instance, 60 per cent of all serious gynaecological problems reported from hospitals are schoolgirl abortions.

Again though in some countries the enrolment levels for both men and women may be roughly equal, the drop out rate for girls is higher. A variety of reasons which include early marriage, pregnancy, parents preferred choices may explain this. Drop out rates among girls in certain countries are as high as 70 per cent.

Related to this issue is the question of literacy. Illiteracy is disproportionately higher in women. On average is sub-Saharan Africa only about 44 per cent of women are literate. Literacy levels are higher amongst males, averaging about 65 per cent. Given the centrality of women's education to health, nutrition and economic growth, surely this ought to be a matter of urgent attention.

Women and Insecurity

Too many problems in the continent are still solved through machetes and guns. The resulting social and political strife explains why one in every three refugees worldwide is an African.

What is frequently ignored in accounts of refugee problems is the fact that most of these are women and children. Aside from the trauma of displacement, they are often crowded into unsanitary refugee camps in the countries into which they flee. Accounts of rapes, sexual violence, general violence and disease epidemics are rampant in all refugee reports that one reads.

Along with the question of refugees we must also look at the fate of internally displaced persons. Poverty, internal strife and rural-urban migration have led to the breakdown of social order. Whether you are in Lusaka, Nairobi, Accra or Addis Ababa, you will encounter street children. Why is this?

Again policy-makers keen to empower women must address the question of internal security. This theme was prominent in the Nairobi Forward Looking Strategies. We must keep hammering it home to policy-makers. I truly cannot overemphasise the importance of internal security to successful empowerment.

Institutions for Implementing Women's Economic Empowerment Policies

Having looked at some key policy areas, what mechanisms exist for the purpose of ensuring that women are not ignored in the process of economic change?

Unfortunately, when one looks across the continent one hardly sees hopeful signs that these matters are receiving urgent attention. We look at only four institutions that to me are important in taking the women agenda on board: the state itself, donors, regional institutions and civil society. I discuss each of these in turn.

The State

The state in Africa has generally been both strong and weak: strong in the areas in which it ought to have been weak and weak in the areas in which it ought to have been strong. Its central features have been a huge centralised bureaucracy and a political elite that generally does not have the welfare of citizens at heart. Two things have been evident in the way the state approaches policy questions that have an impact on women.

First, the state generally lacks a capacity to formulate gender responsive policies. Women are hardly involved at the policy-making levels. They rarely form part of official delegations that discuss economic policies with donors.

Second, on the implementation side, the state does not have the managerial capacity to implement policy. There are several reasons why this is so. The state in Africa has generally been a tool for making money. It has frequently, if not always, been dominated by men. Even the bureaucracy that implements policies has been male dominated. In Kenya, for instance, women have never formed more than 4.7 per cent of the top positions in government. They predominate in the lower cadres where they have no decision-making power.

One of the more urgent reforms clearly is to restructure the state. As part of the democratic agenda, it is important to bring the women's agenda on board. Clearly, in the short run, quick remedies will be necessary. We have in the past argued for affirmative action. This is now more urgent than ever. Certain countries have already moved impressively in this direction. Uganda stands out. But it is the exception. More women are needed in senior positions in government and in politics. In the long run, this would result in a policy-making process that is more gender responsive.

The Donors

The one area in which donors have had a very positive impact is the NGO world. In many marginal areas in Africa health care is still frequently supplied by NGOs. In the political arena, there are human rights organisations doing splendid lobbying work. Much of this work would have been impossible without donor support. I shall have a few remarks to make on this towards the end of the chapter. One of the themes of the Voices from African Women workshop was the whole question of networking. I shall be soon pointing out some things that donors could do in order to move into the next stage of empowering NGOs to carry the women's agenda more effectively.

Regional Institutions

Globalisation and economic integration have become the fashion of the 1990s. GATT has finally converted into the World Trade Organisation. NAFTA is up and running. The European Economic Commission has become the European Union. Former countries of central Europe, Slovenia, the Czech Republic and Poland are all knocking at the door of the European Union seeking admission. In East Africa, we have revived East African Cooperation. In West Africa, there is ECOWAS and the CFA zone. The talk everywhere is about strengthening regional integration.

Where are women in these regional structures? We must explore this question with some attention. The future lies in economic integration. Without attention to the women we just might discover that women are not part of the future into which the world is moving.

Civil Society

The last set of institutions that I wish to discuss are the NGOs and other civil society organisations. These institutions are essential to democratic change. NGOs, churches and trade unions have been crucial in Africa's transition to political pluralism. They were critical in Kenya, Malawi, South Africa, Zambia and elsewhere. What can they do to further the economic empowerment of women? What are some of the ways of enhancing their capacities? I will make some suggestions in the next section about this.

I promised not to be long in this argument. In order to keep my promise I must now very quickly move into some of the areas in which I think there is urgent need for policy reform. What can be done to empower women economically?

The Way Forward

Economic Reforms

The greatest problem with many existing policies is that they have no perspective on women. Specific measures that must be urgently taken include:

- creating an institutional framework that allows for credit to be specifically targeted at women. The existing credit institutions in Africa are not accessible to women. The collateral requirements they impose are out of reach for most women. Where friendly credit institutions exist they are biased towards the formal economy;
- agricultural policies must address the three issues of inputs pricing, land and property ownership and technology and transfer;
- input prices remain high and often out of reach for most small scale farmers. Often the prices of inputs are made high by irrational taxation policies as we have already seen. This is something women must urgently lobby governments to address;
- land ownership and control remain a serious obstacle to women empowerment. Women cannot get loans from banks because they have no collateral. Those who have collateral have no motivation to use their credit on the farm. Each of us can name a few cases in which some man, the registered owner of a parcel of land, has borrowed money on the security of the land and then disappeared into thin air;
- it is important to address the property structure and question of credit simultaneously. Institutions like the African Women's Development Bank are desperately needed. Non-collateral lending is absolutely essential if we are to redress the economic marginalisation of women;
- on technology use, it is now generally recognised that extension services work best if they are specifically targeted at women. Women's capacities to consume technology and use it productively on the land need to be enhanced. Donors' support to agriculture needs to specifically include farmer training programmes that focus on women.

On Political Empowerment

I have already made the point that there is a need for affirmative action programmes in order to bring more women into government. There must be more self-conscious inclusion of women in the civil service bureaucracy.

One of the points that we need to deal with is the question of retrenchment. Retrenchment programmes have a larger impact on women than men. This is partly because women tend to dominate the lower cadres of the civil service. This means that they tend to be the first target of staff cuts. There is, therefore, need for strategies to absorb these women into gainful employment. Such strategies include business skills training and friendly credit schemes.

In addition, laws that hamper women's political participation should be repealed.

On Women's Organisations and Networking

The broad reforms I have pointed out above are however not what I consider most critical. For me, the most important step towards women empowerment is empowering the women themselves to lobby for changes. This means giving internal strength and coherence to women's organisations. We have already mentioned networking. As economies integrate, women's organisations must themselves integrate. What are some of the things that can be done?

Well-wishers and donors willing to support women empowerment must address as a matter of urgency the following key areas.

- First, the need to enhance the managerial capacity of women's organisations. Organisations like the Forum of African Women Educationalists (FAWE), FEMNET and the Council for the Economic Empowerment of Women in Africa (CEEWA) need to have the capacity to lobby. Many times these organisations have to rely on the voluntary services of well-wishers who often have to take time off their own work in other fields. Frequently, the reason for this is that donors have been unwilling to support secretariats and staff working on empowerment programmes. Allow me to be blunt: donors cannot have their cake and eat it. If programme work is going to be professionally done, qualified staff to do this work must be paid for. There are no short cuts in this business.
- There is also the related business of funding training programmes and opportunities for women involved in empowerment work. Often women know where we want to go but sometimes lack the skills to get us there. Some of the skills that they lack include information use techniques, lobbying skills and general organisational and management skills. As we discuss networking and funding we need to address the question of skills and how we can support each other to acquire the skills that can enhance our effectiveness.
- A third crucial area in the empowerment of women is human resource development and utilisation. This is quite different from training people on the job. Let me try and concretise what I have in mind. Frequently research on the condition of the African women is done exclusively by foreign researchers. I think it is important to cut this *intellectual dependency*.

Our friends in the west and in the donor community must not give us fish: they need to give us the capacity to fish. What might they do in this regard?

- First, they need to support the building of indigenous research and consultancy capacities where this capacity does not exist. One of the areas that I see as necessary is to provide capacity in information use and management technology. This is still a relatively new thing in Africa. Only a handful of women have the basic skills to effectively utilise information technology. If we are talking about successful networking, we must develop capacity to use these technologies.
- Second, people who want to support us must show more faith in our consultants and resources. In many cases, we do not have a capacity problem. We often have large numbers of well qualified professionals. In such cases, we have a *capacity utilisation problem*. Our donors and supporters must not participate in the marginalisation of local expertise. They need to show more faith in us and push for increased use of local consultants in gender related research.

Conclusion

There is clearly much more that can be done. And much more that can be discussed. It is clear that our job is cut out for us. The next phase of our efforts is to move towards action. It will not be easy. Some of what we propose sounds futuristic to some of our friends. But we must remember those who fear the future are already dead.

14 Urban and Community Development: Text to Accompany a Video on Women's Networking in Urban Cameroon

DR PAULINE BIYONG
CHAIRPERSON OF THE AFRICAN POVERTY REDUCTION
NETWORK, CAMEROON

Introduction

This chapter is composed of the written text of a video made within the Voices from African Women initiative to demonstrate the infrastructural conditions of urban Cameroon and the role women and women's organisations play in coping with these conditions. The indented text is the voices of Cameroonian women speaking to the difficult nature of their circumstances themselves – the main text is the video commentary.

Urban Planning: the Impact of Women

The population of Cameroon is growing at the rate of three per cent. Although the economic crisis has slowed down rural exodus in recent years, the urban centres have continued to grow too fast for urban planning to keep up with. The majority of neighbourhoods which escape this planning lack social amenities such as potable water.

   In the neighbourhood shown on the video, they are lucky in a way because it is easy to find water without having to dig too deep. In other places, they have to walk a fair distance to fetch water. Some of the wells here are positioned only a few metres away from pit toilets (the video shows this image). Some residents, however, know that this water is not safe to drink as it can carry germs which cause diseases such as typhoid.

Voice of local woman
The water from the well – we use it for laundry and cooking. We always clean the well. It is my husband who looks after it. He always weeds around it and removes any stones. When the water gets dirty, he empties the well. When he fills it up again he disinfects it with bleach and covers it. Two days later, we start using water again. There is no organisation in our neighbourhood for that.

In order to obtain potable water for the family, this woman's husband walks to a pump situated about 12 minutes away from their house. Here he pays five fcca for every 10 litres of the chlorinated water of the national pump company. They would have liked to receive pipe-borne water from this network but they cannot afford the cost because the husband is unemployed.

Voice of local women's leader
There are families, communities and individuals who get together to fix drinking water points in their neighbourhoods, otherwise they get into contact with SNEC to get connected up with the national water company. The government has created public taps where water has to be paid for but not everybody can afford it and so women are still leaving their houses to fetch water. The problem of potable water provision is also a problem of education. There are public taps which the government and sometimes the community have installed at a high cost but which have been damaged by these same communities.

Life in recent years is also marked by a severe economic crisis. At the level of individuals, this has meant increased poverty and a high level of unemployment, even after graduating from university. The burden of this poverty has fallen squarely on the shoulders of the women, they in many cases become the sole breadwinners of their families, ensuring that children and husbands survive from day to day. Many sell groceries and have to work extremely long hours for very little profit. Some of these women come from the villages with their goods and if they do not sell everything by nightfall then they are obliged to spend the night beside their goods – they can not return to the village with all this load. 60 per cent of the grocery market is controlled by women. (The video show shots of the women traders and their uncomfortable circumstances.)

Voices of women traders
Those who live in town have to be up early to secure goods to sell at daybreak.

We have to leave our houses at 4 a.m. to go and scramble for produce at the back of vehicles from the villages.

Those who sell groceries sometimes end up having nothing to sell just because they did not work up early enough.

Our greatest problem is transportation – we don't have the means to go to the village to buy produce. Those who trade in fish have difficulty arriving at their destinations with the fish in a good state. Sometimes they arrive when the cold store is already closed – they themselves do not own cold stores – and by the morning, the fish has started decomposing. So sometimes they sell it at a loss because they lack facilities for preservation.

These problems point to a need to develop market infrastructures, The authorities have made an effort to build markets, yet most of these structures remain unoccupied.

Voice of woman trader
The counters are very small. Even goods at 20,000 frs cfa won't fit into them. The counters are too narrow. Two people can't sit back to back in them. So since we used to place our goods on the ground, customers go for those who place their goods on the ground. When you're on the counters, you don't get any customers.

(The video shows a group of women.) This group of women meet monthly. Each one of them contributes a fixed amount of money and the total is given to one of the members – each member has her turn. It is like an interest free loan.

Voice of a woman group member
The majority of the members of Oyili Nnem Mboh are 'buyam sellams', that is retailers. The aim of our association is to promote understanding and collaboration between its members. This is in order to satisfy our common interests, and to help each other out in happy and unhappy events. In the association, we save money and this helps in our business activities.

Such associations can be used as a base for organising commercial activities. In some markets, the women have formed distribution and retail networks to sell their produce.

Voice of local women's leader

In order to take the role of women into consideration in urban planning, it is necessary to organise their activities both in the villages and in the towns. For example, set up structures of storage and distribution in the markets. This will have the advantage of reducing the amount of time the women spend out of their homes, so that they can pay more attention to childcare.

The poorest members of the population visit health centres only as a last resort.

And as if in response to a certain need, many medical staff are setting up private clinics in their neighbourhoods. It is necessary for these practitioners to have the honesty to recognise where their role ends and that of a qualified doctor begins.

Voice of local female health worker

Two days ago, I was called upon at 2 a.m. in the morning because a young girl was having an abortion about two houses away from here. I told them that such a case as this one ought to be taken to a hospital. I helped to get the placenta out and gave her an injection of antibiotics which I had – luckily. She was supposed to pay for this but she did not – she promised to pay later. I'm in contact with lots of people – especially the women. They come to me with their health problems and those of their children. Until recently things were easy – because people had money and I saw them in health centres. Actually, few people visit health centres nowadays because they do not have the money. It costs money to consult a doctor and the prescriptions are very expensive, so they can not afford it. They consult medical personnel at home, or buy medicines from hawkers, and it is a big problem because they don't treat themselves properly. For urban development, I think we should take health care to the people. I think the best thing to do would be to find them in their groups. There are religious groups in all parishes and also many non-religious groups in various neighbourhoods and even markets, where women meet every month or every week. If the time can be found to talk to these women, then they will listen. The women I receive here – first of all, I can't consult because I am not a doctor, so I mostly give advice: advice on what to do, when to see a doctor, how to care for children, what to eat.

Conclusion

Considering women's roles in urban planning implies providing appropriate infrastructures. It is also necessary for women to associate with each other in groups to improve the quality of life in their communities. Already in several neighbourhoods in Cameroon, women's organisations are getting involved in activities such as neighbourhood clean up campaigns.

(Editors' note: The video and its text has taken us through a number of critical areas of women's needs and organisations in urban life. Commencing with the need for improvements in water supply, the video has taken us into the areas of involving women in the better design of markets so as to meet their storage and selling needs, into the area of the need for improvements in transportation and distribution systems for female traders, into the microfinance arrangements and needs of women's groups and finishes by taking us into the need for decentralised health services for women. The areas covered by the video make the case for the direct inclusion of women in the urban planning of the services for which they are the main users.)

15 Agricultural Opportunities and Constraints in Rural Nigeria: A Gender Perspective

ESTHER SUSUYU MBANYIMAN
HADEJA-NGURU WETLANDS CONSERVATION PROJECT, KANO,
NIGERIA

Introduction

As part of the Voices from African Women initiative, gender networking was undertaken with girls and women in rural Africa on issues relevant to gender and agriculture. I wish to express my appreciation to all the communities, especially the women who took time from their busy schedules to participate in the village meetings. I particularly thank them for their patience in answering all my questions. I extend my thanks also to the village heads for giving me the permission to hold meetings in their villages on short notice. Under the Voices initiative, the task was to establish networking in Nigeria in the field of agriculture at the village level in line with the African Platform for Action and the Beijing Platform for action. The emphasis was on identifying existing opportunities and constraints in agriculture, gender and development in Nigeria and raising awareness of these issues. The central question is how village communities see the current disparities in gender roles and where they think the opportunities are for bridging the gap towards equality. To achieve this, networking materials developed by the Technical Department of the World Bank in Washington (Appendix 1) were selected as focal points for discussion with village communities, extensionists, local experts and industrialists.

There is a disparity in culture, attitude and approach to issues amongst people in different parts of Nigeria. However, people from the north have a lot of similarities and so do people from the south. There are three dominant cultures/tribes in the country – the Ibo, Hausa and Yoruba – spreading across the country in the south, north and west respectively. The way other people from minority tribes within these regions think and behave is influenced by the culture of the three tribes. People from the middle belt – Tivs, Birom, etc. – seem to have a combination of cultures that is slightly influenced by all the dominant tribes.

To make this study representative, data has to be collected from different parts of the country. Thus, the country was divided into five zones, namely, the east, west, middle belt, central and northern zones. Nine villages spread across the five zones were purposively selected and data was collected using informal, participatory group meetings. One village was selected from the western, eastern, middle belt and central zones while five villages were selected from the northern zone because it is considered to have a larger land area than the other zones.

In two of the nine villages, key informants provided all the information, while in seven, data were collected using informal, participatory community meetings. In each village, six participatory meetings were held with an average of 20 participants in each group: the six groups were women's group, men's group, girls' group, boys' group, mixed boys' and girls' group, mixed men's and women's group.

At each of the meetings, participants were asked to enumerate what they considered as women's and men's as well as boys' and girls' tasks in agriculture/household chores. Later, they were asked to say who does more work, women or men, girls or boys and how these tasks can be shared equally between men/women and girls/boys. The mixed group meetings were meant to confirm the information provided by the single sex groups.

Discussions during the meetings were largely open, although sometimes, the discussions were guided by questions developed centring around the selected sections of the networking materials.

In all the villages, women were asked during group meetings to identify female-headed households. Later, key informants (male) were also asked to provide the same information.

Person-to-person discussions were held with industrialists, local experts and extensionists. In towns in all the zones, an informal meeting was held with key informants. The informants, who were themselves female-headed households,[1] were identified through their ward heads.

Outcome of the Meetings

Female-headed Households by Zones and their Specific Problems in Terms of Economic and Food Security

Zones without female-headed households From the information available, there were no female-headed households in the villages selected from the central and western zones. Similarly, four of the five villages selected in the northern zone (Gasma, Rumfankara, Mallindi and Maijigila) had no female-headed households. Only two divorced women were found in Gasma, one divorced for one year, the other one for two years. The former is living with, and being provided for, by her father; the latter by her brother. Both are intending to get married soon. None of them is farming nor living with their children.

This means, in most rural areas of Nigeria, it is uncommon to find a woman who has no husband, lives alone with her children, manages the family and the farm and has sole responsibility for providing and/or taking decisions in the house. They tend to remarry as soon as they are divorced or widowed. A divorced woman goes back to her family, taking only children who are very young (1–4 years old). The husband is expected to provide feeding allowance for the children. When the wife prepares to remarry, the former husband decides whether or not to allow the lady to keep their children. It is, however, very common in the villages to find women who are de facto household heads as their husbands are away from home once in a while. Whilst the husbands are away, the women are responsible for making some of the decisions in the family with most input from their husbands' relatives or the husband's messages.

Variations to this phenomenon were found amongst some minority tribes. For instance, Shuwa (a Marghi village in the north), have women who decide not to remarry but stay to raise their children. Other tribes are the Bura of southern Borno State, Bachama of Taraba State, Kilba of Adamawa State and Kaje of Kaduna state.

Zones with female-headed households There are large numbers of female-headed households in the middle belt and eastern zones. In Du (the village studied in the middle belt), 30 out of a total of 300 households are female-headed. In the eastern zone, however, female-headed households are obliged by tradition to rely heavily on the opinion of the elder and/or younger brothers of their late husbands to arrive at a decision in all matters.

In most towns/cities in all the zones, some of the western-educated women decide to stay alone and raise their children after divorce or loss of a husband. Some feel strongly against being married. They choose to get pregnant out of wedlock, keep the father of the child anonymous, and raise their own families. This phenomenon seems to cut across all cultures. Women in this group have paid jobs in government/non-governmental or private institutions. Some have personal businesses. They take all the decisions in the family. Problems experienced as identified by each of the different groups are highlighted below.

Specific Problems in Terms of Economic and Food Security

Rural women: single-headed households and de facto female-headed households identified the following problems.

- Having multiple roles, hence, less time and energy to give adequate attention to any particular role.
- Inability to cultivate and manage large areas of farmland due to lack of money to purchase and/or hire farm implements for land preparation and weeding.
- Inability to acquire inputs such as fertiliser or where available, improved seeds.
- Lack of access to credit, especially those from formal sources such as the banks due to lack of collateral.
- Having to forego some essential needs in order to solve other pressing issues. For example, one woman pointed out her daughter, who was coming from a neighbour's house where she had fetched fire on a cornstalk. The mother could not buy matches because she needed the money to buy some aspirin for her son who had a headache.

Educated women: single-headed households and de facto female-headed households identified the following problems.

- Having multiple roles, hence, less time and energy to give adequate attention to any particular role.
- Non-recognition in the society, hence lack of confidence to venture into anything.
- Only one source of income which has to be spread thinly.
- Inability to acquire better education and/or jobs because they can not leave their children behind.
- Discrimination by institutions, organisations and parastatals because they

do not want to incur extra costs of accepting responsibility of women's children.

Institutional Opportunities for Representatives of Female-headed Households to Participate in Development Dialogue and in Planning

A number of institutions that could offer opportunities for female-headed households to participate in development dialogue and planning were identified through the group meetings. Opportunities for rural women and educated women were seen as being somewhat different. For rural women in single-headed households and de facto female-headed households the following opportunities could be targeted.

- Membership of village development organisations/associations. As members, they will be able to influence the type of programmes identified and/or undertaken by the organisation.
- Membership of village councils. Membership will allow them to formulate policies that address issues that meet their specific needs.
- Women's cooperatives. Membership will allow them to obtain credit or relevant information/assistance.
- Rural community banks. Membership will allow them to obtain credit.
- The Federal Government of Nigeria's family support programme. Membership will allow them to benefit from the programme's activities.

For educated women the following opportunities could be targeted.

- Political institutions such as the House of Representatives – where national policies are formulated.
- Pressure groups/lobbyist: to influence organisations' opinion in favour of the women.
- The news media: to provide information which will raise awareness amongst the general populace on the needs of these group of women and to rally support for positive actions.
- Formal banks: to obtain credit.

Relevant Extension Messages for Women

Extension leaflets have relevant messages for women. However, the messages are presented in such a way that frequently render them useless for women. This is because most rural women are illiterate and are hardly visited by extension agents. The materials are too technical, long and sometimes inaccessible. In some cases, they are written under the assumption that there are sufficient extension agents around to carry the messages to the end users whereas there are not.

Considering the household responsibilities, time and resource constraints of rural women, the extension messages listed in Appendix 2 to this chapter are of relevance to Nigerian rural women – there is need, however, for their messages to be converted into knowledge useable by females involved in agriculture through better gender targeted extension practices.

Existing Differences in Land Ownership and Use Rights According to Gender

Technically, the Nigerian Land Use Act of 1979 allows every citizen of Nigeria to have access to land and/or own it. Similarly, Islamic and Christian laws give all members of the family opportunity to inherit family lands. These notwithstanding, implementation of the act and the laws are influenced by all cultures. In most cases they tend to be biased towards men.

Rural women are unaware of the existence of the Land Use Act. They have access to land as long as they remain married. The land is owned by their husbands. When they are divorced, they lose access to any pieces of land they were cultivating in the past. They have access to their relatives'/ family land until they remarry. The consensus is that there are no problems with having access to land. But there are a lot of problems in wanting to own land. It is not common for young women to inherit land. In exceptional cases, land can be given by the family to an older woman of 50 and above who decides to leave her husband's family to come home to her relatives. The woman will have sole control over that land. She can trade it, lend it, sell it, etc. Young women who can afford and have the desire to own land will have to acquire/purchase the land under the names of their brothers or male relatives. Sometimes, the male relatives cheat by declaring the land as theirs. It is impossible to contest it in court because the papers are made out in the relatives' names.

Rural men can own land. They acquire land through inheritance and/or purchase of one. Those who are migrants can purchase or hire land for as long as they reside in the new village.

Town (educated) men and women are aware of the land laws. They can have access to and own lands. It is, however, more difficult for women to acquire land due to the complexities and bureaucratic delays inherent in the processes of acquiring land in the country. Another problem for women is how to fulfil some of the conditions laid out in the Land Use Act. For example, the Act allows '5000ha of land for farming or grazing ...'. Although many women will want to have 5000ha for farming or grazing, very few of them can raise enough money to pay for the stipulated 5000ha.

There are no differences in land rights amongst the various cultural groups of the country. In all cases, women have access to land that belongs to their husbands or relatives. Land is primarily owned by men. It is easier for men to purchase land than it is for women, even if women have enough money to buy it.

Mechanisms for Change as Perceived by Local Women and Local Experts

Agents of change as identified by local women and local experts are:

- education: broadens a someone's mind and gives him/her the ideas for change;
- contact with people from other cultures: shows someone different ways of doing things;
- contact with the towns, cities and other countries (Mecca and Jerusalem): shows some one different ways of doing things;
- advertisements on the radio (BBC, Radio Kaduna/Lagos): shows some one different ways of doing things;
- having enough money: makes it possible for someone to participate in change;
- government policies.

Opportunities for Sharing Household Workloads Equitably Between Females and Males, Girls and Boys

Gender Disparity in Workloads

In most of the villages studied, participants agreed that women and girls have more tasks than men and boys. This is also true for women and girls in the towns (educated women and girls attending school). An exception is Mallindi (one of the five villages from the northern zone), men and boys do more work than women and girls. This is because over 90 per cent of the families keep their wives in purdah (a Moslem tenet that restricts the movement of women outside the home). The primary roles of the majority of women in this community is food preparation and washing dishes.

To share tasks equally between young boys and girls, it was suggested by boys', girls' and women's groups that parents (both father and mother) share family responsibilities between girls and boys without reference to their sex. Parents should ensure that each person does his or her task even if it means forcing them. When they grow up, they will see each other as equals and they will not see tasks in relation to sex. In the case of older boys and girls, it was suggested that discussions be held between each family so as to identify what is acceptable to them.

Older men and women cannot think of any ways of getting husbands to personally share household chores. One woman even exclaimed 'Won't he divorce you if you asked him to help with household chores?'. To reduce the burden on women, it was implied that men take on some of the traditionally female roles in agriculture.

Men in the towns are prepared to share responsibilities if they can find time for it and provided the women ask them to help. Here, the emphasis is on the women asking; but most women do not ask because that is translated to mean they are incapable of coping, so they are therefore afraid to be seen as bad housewives.

Technological Improvements to Lessen Workload

The following interventions were listed as means to lessen women's workload.

- Ox teams or tractors for land preparation.
- Implements for weeding.
- Implements for threshing.
- Availability of inputs such as fertiliser and/or improved seeds.
- Implements for dehusking and grinding grains.
- Implements for moving water from the water point to the house.
- Implements that use less firewood.
- Implements for processing palm fruits into palm oil and palm kernels into vegetable oil.

- Implements for processing cassava, yams, and potatoes into gari, flour and flour respectively.

Moving Rural Industrialisation Programmes Forward

According to extensionists, industrialists are profit-oriented. To attract them to site industries in villages, the government and its parastatals have to make some input and efforts such as:

- compiling an inventory of what is available in villages;
- conducting research to identify existing opportunities for what has been identified in the inventory;
- put rural infrastructure in place;
- give tax breaks for industries based on their location, with those located in villages having the highest break;
- provide financial support to progressive industries that are prepared to site in the villages.

Overall, rural women see the chances to obtain industries in rural areas through the lobbying of governments by a very strong and influential man who is sympathetic towards them. The idea is to get the government to site industries in villages where there are appropriate raw materials, giving them the following mandates:

- food production;
- food processing;
- production of medicines from herbs and trees;
- processing of raw materials for bigger industries.

Recommendations

The following recommendations emerged out of discussions with grassroots women and are given with the purpose of alleviating the constraints of rural women and girls and to give them the opportunity to participate in development initiatives.

- Identify and promote on-shelf, location-specific technologies for household tasks and weeding. This will lessen women's tasks and release their time for other things including leisure.
- Identify and promote on-shelf, location-specific technologies for processing agricultural products such as palm fruits, groundnuts, cassava, maize, etc. at the village level.
- Provide financial and technical support for agricultural development to female-headed households.
- Support and sponsor women's participation in policy-formulating institutions at all levels of government such as membership of the village council, house of assembly, house of representatives, etc.
- Support female education through award of scholarships.
- Support the development of information centres on the location and availability of industrial raw materials.
- Develop and support an awareness campaign in villages on the disadvantages of division of tasks based on sex.
- Support awareness campaigns amongst rural women on the existence and conditions in the Nigerian Land Use Act.
- Support awareness campaigns amongst rural women on their rights as laid down in religious books – men respect and observe the tenets of religion better.
- Support the development of rural infrastructure.

Observations and Conclusions

Women were more open and prepared to talk about everything in their individual groups than in the mixed groups. Most of them kept quiet and assumed a subservient position when men were around. On the other hand, men talked more when the women were around. The men even pretended that they had discussed women's needs in their individual groups.

Female-headed households are virtually nonexistent in most rural areas, especially in the predominantly Moslem areas of the north. However, it is common to find them amongst minority tribes. These minority tribes are predominantly Christians. This probably means that Moslem women are under bigger pressure to remarry than Christian women.

Female-headed households from the eastern and western zones seem to have fewer tasks and problems than their counterparts in the other zones. This is because their ex-husbands' relatives make a lot of input to family matters, including taking decisions on children's school attendance. However, they are less happy, as they cannot take sole initiative even in situations where they are convinced of the positive outcome of their intended actions. The relatives take credit for everything that happens in the family, with or without concrete input. Therefore the women feel reluctant to take personal initiatives.

In all the zones, there are only superficial opportunities for female-headed households to participate in development dialogues and planning unless they have a lot of wealth. Most of the institutional opportunities identified during the discussion do not function well in women's favour. For instance, women's cooperatives are not available in most villages; rural community banks are not very effective because of the culture of embezzlement by bank officials. The Federal Government of Nigeria's Family Support Programme is dominated by few 'educated' women who have little or no experience of interacting with rural women and the funds are often embezzled by the chairladies.

Extension leaflets have relevant messages for women. However, the messages are presented in such a way that render them useless for women. This is because most rural women are illiterate and are hardly visited by extension agents. The materials are too technical, long and sometimes inaccessible. In some cases, they are written under the assumption that they are sufficient extension agents around to carry the messages to the end users where as there are not.

Changes occur faster in villages that are accessible and/or closer to cities. Even women in purdah hear more things and are more aware if their husbands live in villages that are accessible. Education, for both adults and young people seem to be the only passport to appreciating and assimilating changes with in villages.

Women hardly see their tasks in the farm and the house as jobs or contributing to anything. In all the zones, the first answer one gets when you ask 'who does more work in the farm/house?', is 'men'. But if one considers the list of what men do and what women do, you end up asking for more fingers to put women's tasks on as against those of men. Asked why they said men did more work: 'Because their job is heavier and more difficult'. This is interesting because, for instance, in the eastern and western zones, women are responsible for carrying all the yams, on their heads, from the farm to the house and weeding through out the farming season. But still they think that making yam heaps and harvesting it (men's tasks) are heavier. It does not occur to them that they hardly have time for leisure. When they come back from the farm, the men sit or lie under the tree, while women are busy cooking or processing food. It is beyond women to ask men to share household tasks with them. Some cannot even comprehend the idea. They are afraid of being divorced as a result of such actions; or of being viewed as an incompetent wife. In some villages, the women's group said 'only God can touch their heart to help us'. Technological improvements to lessen women's tasks are necessary and urgent. This is particularly true for female-headed households.

Extension agents think that a lot needs to be done before rural industrialisation can be moved forward. According to them, the responsibility for creating a favourable environment for rural industrialisation rests with a government. Rural women see opportunities for industrialisation mainly in food production and food processing, while the urban sector sees it in terms of provision of infrastructure and tax breaks.

The Land Use Act allows women rights of land ownership, but this has not been so in practice. In all the zones, women have access to land but not ownership rights. Men on the other hand have ownership rights regardless of whether they use the land or not. Purchase of land is much easier for men than for women. It is therefore essential to make women aware of their rights under the land use act.

Education, contact with people from other cultures, the news media, availability of money and government policies have been identified as the major mechanisms for change by women in all zones.

Note

1 For the purpose of this task, a female-headed household is defined as 'a productive unit made up of a female (with or without de facto husband), her children and/or relatives sharing food from the same cooking pot'.

References and Background Reading

Abdullahi, A.H. and Mbanyiman, E.S. (1993) (eds), *Report on Technical Workshop on Donkey Draught Technology*, report to Hadejia-Nguru Wetlands Conservation Project, 6 pp.

Asubonteng, K.O., Le Quoc, D., Liem, K., Mbanyiman, E.S., Meindertsma, D., Medrano, W. and Simpungwe, E. (1994), *Improvement of Agricultural Systems in the Drylands of Indonesia: the case of Sumba*, ICRA working document series No. 36, Indonesia.

Kwara Agricultural Development Project (undated), *Soyabeans Utilisation*, Extension Guide No. 1 revised edition), publications of the Extension Department, Kwara Agricultural Development Project, Illorin, Nigeria.

Kwara Agricultural Development Project (undated), *Maize Production*. Bulletin No. 1, Illorin, Nigeria.

Mbanyiman, E.S. (1994), *Women: the real workforce*, paper prepared and submitted for consideration to FEMCONSULT (Consultants on Women and Development), The Hague, the Netherlands.

Mbanyiman, E.S. (1991), *Comparative Performance of Woodstoves (Clay Type) with the tree stone open fire system at Karasuwa Garun Guna, Yobe State, Nigeria*, report to North East Arid Zone Development Project, Gashua, Nigeria, 9 pp.

National Agricultural Extension and Research Liaison Services, Federal Ministry of Agriculture and Natural Resources in collaboration with the Institute for Agricultural Research (IAR) (1981), *Guide on the Control of Smut Diseases on Guinea Corn*, Extension Guide No. 52, Ahmadu Bello University Zaria, Nigeria.

National Agricultural Extension and Research Liaison Services, Federal Ministry of Agriculture and Natural Resources in collaboration with the Institute for Agricultural Research (IAR) (1976), *The Management of Broilers*, Extension Guide No. 4, Ahmadu Bello University Zaria, Nigeria.

National Agricultural Extension and Research Liaison Services, Federal Ministry of Agriculture and Natural Resources in collaboration with the Institute for Agricultural Research (IAR) (undated), *Guide to the Production of Carrots*, Extension Guide No. 39, Ahmadu Bello University Zaria, Nigeria.

National Agricultural Extension and Research Liaison Services, Federal Ministry of Agriculture and Natural Resources in collaboration with the Institute for Agricultural Research (IAR) (1987), *Guide to Personal Hygiene*, Extension Guide No. 138, Ahmadu Bello University Zaria, Nigeria.

National Agricultural Extension and Research Liaison Services, Federal Ministry of Agriculture and Natural Resources in collaboration with the Institute for Agricultural Research (IAR) (1994), *Recommended Practices for Groundnut Production*, Extension Recommended Practices No. 1, Ahmadu Bello University Zaria, Nigeria.

National Agricultural Extension and Research Liaison Services, Federal Ministry of Agriculture and Natural Resources in collaboration with the Institute for Agricultural Research (IAR), *Guide on the Production of Soyabean in Nigeria*, Extension Guide No. 3, Ahmadu Bello University Zaria, Nigeria.

National Agricultural Technology Support Projects – The Kano State Agricultural and Rural Development Authority (1994), *Agronomic Recommendations for Wet Season Crops*. Technical Guide No. 2, Kano State Agricultural and Rural Development Authority.

National Fadama Development Projects (undated), *Agronomic Recommendations for Fadama Crops*, Technical Guide No. 1, the Kano State Agricultural and Rural Development Authority.

Nigerian Stored Products Research Institute, *Storing your produce*, Advisory Booklet Series for: Maize; Yams; Cassava, etc., published by the Nigerian Stored Products Research Institute, Lagos.

Palte, H.D. (1992), *Farming UNLtd?! Quest for appropriate oil conservation in Ibo land.*

Appendix 1 Selected Sections of Networking Material Adapted from the African Platform for Action and the Beijing Platform for Action

Networking on gender and agriculture in Nigeria can be built around the recommendations of the African Platform for Action and the Beijing Platform for action. Key recommendations are given below with a supporting package of local actions that can be taken to move these recommendations towards implementation.

Formulate and Implement Specific Economic, Food Security and Related Policies in Support of Female-headed Households

- Identify a set of female-headed households by region and ask them to identify the specific problems they face in terms of economic and food security.
- Identify institutional opportunities for representatives of female-headed households to participate in the development dialogue and in planning.
- Identify a set of extension messages which have particular relevance for women given their household responsibilities, time and resource constraints.

Provide Land Rights on an Equitable Basis for Women and Men in Terms of Ownership and Utilisation and Monitor Implementation

- Identify existing differences in land ownership and use rights.
- Identify mechanisms for change as perceived by local women and local experts.
- Establish whether there are substantial differences between women's land rights within the various regions and amongst the various cultural groups of the country.

Reduce Girls' and Women's Workload Through, Among Others Things, Provision of Appropriate Technologies for all Aspects of Farming and Household Tasks

- Discuss with local girls and women the opportunities for sharing household workloads more equitably between females and males, girls and boys.

- Discuss with local women what technological opportunities would lessen their load.

Promote Rural Industrialisation Schemes, Thus Reducing Rural/Urban Migration Through the Participation of Women in the Design, Development, Promotion and Dissemination of Food Technologies

- Discuss with the extension service how this programme can be moved forward.
- Discuss with rural women and urban business sector, e.g. food industry, where they see opportunities for rural industrialisation.

Appendix 2 Extension Literature for Rural Women in Nigeria

Guide on the production of soyabean in Nigeria, Extension Guide No. 3 (1994), publications of the National Agricultural Extension and Research Liaison Services: Federal Ministry of Agricultural and Natural Resources in collaboration with the Institute for Agricultural Research (IAR), Ahmadu bello University Zaria, Nigeria.

Recommended practices for groundnut production, Extension Recommended Practices No. 1 (1994), publications of the National Agricultural Extension and Research Liaison Services: Federal Ministry of Agricultural and Natural Resources in collaboration with the Institute for Agricultural Research (IAR), Ahmadu bello University Zaria, Nigeria.

Guide to personal hygiene, Extension Guide No. 138 (1987), publications of the National Agricultural Extension and Research Liaison Services: Federal Ministry of Agricultural and Natural Resources in collaboration with the Institute for Agricultural Research (IAR), Ahmadu bello University Zaria, Nigeria.

Guide to the production of carrots, Extension Guide No. 39 (undated), publications of the National Agricultural Extension and Research Liaison Services: Federal Ministry of Agricultural and Natural Resources in collaboration with the Institute for Agricultural Research (IAR), Ahmadu bello University Zaria, Nigeria.

Guide on the control of smut disease on guinea corn, Extension guide No. 52 (1981), publications of the National Agricultural Extension and Research Liaison Services: Federal Ministry of Agricultural and Natural Resources in collaboration with the Institute for Agricultural Research (IAR), Ahmadu bello University Zaria, Nigeria.

The management of broilers, Extension Guide No. 4 (1976), publications of the National Agricultural Extension and Research Liaison Services: Federal Ministry of Agricultural and Natural Resources in collaboration with the Institute for Agricultural Research (IAR), Ahmadu bello University Zaria, Nigeria.

Soya beans utilisation, Extension Guide No. 1 (revised edition) (undated), publications of the Extension Department, Kwara Agricultural Development Project, Illorin, Nigeria.

Maize production, Bulletin No. 1 (undated), publications of the Extension Department, Kwara Agricultural Development Project, Illorin, Nigeria.

Agronomic recommendation for wet season crops, Technical guide No. 2 (1994), National Agricultural Technology Support Projects – the Kano State Agricultural and Rural Development Authority.

Agronomic recommendations for fadama crops, Technical guide No. 1 (undated), National Fadama Development Projects – the Kano State Agricultural and Rural Development Authority.

Nigerian Stored Products Research Institute, *Storing your produce*, Advisory Booklet series for: maize; yams; cassava, etc. , published by the Nigerian Stored Products Research Institute, Lagos.

16 Education and the Girl Child: Evidence from Ghana

PROFESSOR NANA ARABA APT
DIRECTOR OF THE CENTRE FOR SOCIAL POLICY STUDIES,
UNIVERSITY OF GHANA AND CHAIRPERSON OF RESPONSE (AN
NGO FOR STREET CHILDREN)

Introduction

The 'girl child' is a major component of the African Platform for Action. Policy-makers, women's organisations and African academics have come to focus on the disproportionate burden of domestic work carried by girls and the educational disadvantage this imposes upon the African girl child. Girl drop-out rates from school are a major problem in many African countries and Ghana shares in this pattern of female educational loss. RESPONSE, a Ghanaian NGO dedicated to improving the circumstances of Ghana's street children, has been active in identifying the social and economic situations which bring the girl children of Ghana into urban areas as head load porters (kayayoos), petty traders and maidservants. Under the Voices from African Initiative, RESPONSE and the Centre for Social Policy Studies, University of Ghana, research was undertaken to identify the precise circumstances under which girl children drop out of education. This document contains a collection of 'voices' of girls who dropped out of school in Bimbilla, the district capital of Nanumba in the Northern Region of Ghana. They tell their own stories giving the reasons why they left school. Interviews were conducted in the local dialect and literal translations made as close as possible to the girls' own expressions. The question put to them was simple: What made them leave school?

The methodology was also simple. Class registers of a selected year group from Primary School Grade 1–6 and Junior Secondary School Grade 1–3 were examined to find out the girl drop-outs at each stage. 82 girl drop-outs were identified in a 10 year period from 1986. With assistance of teachers and classmates of identified girl drop-outs, 25 of this number were tracked down in the Northern Region and interviewed. Interestingly enough, four of them were located in the capital city, Accra, portering at the Agbogbloshie market.

Bimbilla occupies a land space of about three square kilometres. It has an estimated population of about 15,500 inhabitants, according to the last census figures of 1984. About 96 per cent are Nanumbas and natives of the land.

Predominantly, the people are farmers practising subsistence agriculture. They cultivate crops such as maize, millet, groundnuts, cotton, cassava, pepper, beans and above all yam is Bimbilla's major cash crop. Farming in this area engages the work time of both the male and female population. Women and girls are mostly engaged with the harvesting of the above crops except yam. They are also responsible for transporting the farm produce to the market for sale. Quite apart from these, they are charged with the responsibility of household care and domestic management.

Voices

Akosua (18 years) left school at the age of 13

I left school because I had no money to pay for my school fees. My father who is responsible for my education died immediately I entered Junior Secondary School. My mother wanted me to assist her to educate my brothers.

Prisila (15 years) left school at the age of 14

I left school due to pregnancy. I wanted to get money to enable me to acquire some of my school needs.

Arija (17 years) left school at the age of 14

I was fed up with the education and the school subjects are too many and difficult. To confess, I did not have interest in school.

Bushira (19 years) left school at the age of 15

I left school due to financial constraints. I could not pay my school fees, buy books and other requirements. My father is old and cannot do any serious farming to support us. I think through my work now I can assist my mother.

Fati (16 years) left school at the age of 13

I could not pay my school fees and was sent home.

Mary (15 years) left school at the age of 14

I could not afford to pay my fees. My table was also stolen and I had no money to buy one. Without the table I could not go back to school as the headmaster insisted.

Aramatu (15 years) left school at the age of 13

I want to learn how to trade. I do not like school because in the end I will end up not going any further. After all I think people go to school with the ultimate objective of earning a better life. But I think education is brain cracking, time consuming and frustrating. I therefore prefer doing business.

Salamatu (18 years) left school at the age of 14

School is difficult. Moreover I know that because I am a girl I will not go high. And my father does not want to pay my school fee. Only that of my brothers. My mother can not pay the school fees of my brother and me. One brother is in JSS 3 and the others in primary school. She wants me to assist her to support my brothers.

Aisha (15 years) left school at the age of 15

I have no table to use. The one I had was stolen. My parents (especially my father) do not encourage me by buying me the table. Without the table I cannot attend classes hence my being at home.

Hindu (17 years) left school at the age of 15

I left school due to pregnancy. I had no help hence I took a boyfriend to help me. My father has 39 children. So I only receive help from my mother and my boy friend. I help my mother's children through my boy friend who is a worker.

Amina (19 years) left school at the age of 14

I dropped out due to the pregnancy. This was due to the need to take responsibility for my school needs.

Fusheina (15 years) left school at the age of 13

I could not pay my school fees. I was therefore sent home. My father prefers my brothers' education to mine. I do not know why this is so but I think he is thinking a girl should be prepared for marriage.

Afishetu (17 years) left school at the age of 14

I left school because I do not like school. I love to learn a trade. Through this I will get money and assets to be respectfully married.

Lubaba (19 years) left school at the age of 17

I left school just to marry. I do not want to bring shame to my parents as girls in this area do. Currently I am pregnant.

Akosua (17 years) left school at the age of 15

I was sacked from school due to pregnancy. Because of the need to get assistance outside my home, I ended my school like this (being pregnant).

Bintu (18 years) left school at the age of 14

I was removed from school by my father. He said girls do not perform well when they are sent to school in this area and so he would not waste money for nothing fruitful. My mother is also not capable of sponsoring me though the will is there.

Furera (14 years) left school at the age of 14

My parents could not pay my school fees and I was sent home from school.

Ayi (19 years) left school at the age of 15

I left school to learn sewing as the school was boring. I never understood what was being taught in class.

Balia (20 years) left school at the age of 16

I was removed and married off to my husband. I did not want to disobey my parents, so I do their wish.

Samira (19 years) left school at the age of 15

I left school because of pregnancy. I needed money to supplement my parents efforts so I took a boyfriend. Little did I know it will end my education.

Balchisu (16 years) left school at the age of 15

This was due to the ethnic conflict between the Konkombas and Nanumbas. I was brought here (Accra) to my sister, that is my aunt's daughter, to work so that I can get money to assist my parents at home and the family. Through this I may also accumulate money to prepare myself towards marriage. I work as a kayayoo in Agbogbloshie market.

Rakia (17 years) left school at the age of 15

My parents could not pay my school fees and so I was sent here (Accra) to my aunt to work. On arrival I discovered there was no work even for my aunt and life was no better either for her. I saw my colleagues in the kaya business and decided to join them.

Ponaa (19 years) left school at the age of 16

I left school due to pregnancy. After my safe delivery, I saw that life was not easy for my parent neither was it easy for me, so I came to Accra. I am here working as a porter to acquire certain basic things as a wife since the war has claimed all of our assets. After six months I hope to return home to Bimbilla.

Damata (19 years) left school at the age of 16

I wanted to learn sewing or to become a seamstress. However my parents could not acquire me a sewing machine. I therefore left school and home for Accra have to work to acquire the machine the machine and return home. I am porter (kayayoo).

Memunatu (20 years) left school at the age of 13

I left school to learn a trade. However, as I had no initial capital I came to Accra to work as a kayayoo to accumulate money to fulfil my vision.

Conclusion

There are a number of key issues which emerge out of listening to these girl child voices.

- The labour and earning of girls is used to support the education of boys.
- School fees represent a strong barrier to the education of girls.
- Girls do not view the current school curriculum as useful in the development of occupational skills.
- Pregnancy and/or marriage are major reasons for girls dropping out of schools.

Key policy approaches which can be used to address these issues are:

- the development of strong information, education and communication campaigns designed to encourage households to keep their girls at school;
- provide girls with scholarships;
- permit girls to return to school after pregnancy;
- develop curricula, teaching methods and timing of education which are more appropriate to the circumstances of the girl child.

Further Reading

Agarwal, S., Attah, M., Apt, N.A., Grieco, M.S., Kwakye, E.A. and Turner, J. (1997), 'Bearing the weight: the kayayoo, Ghana's girl working child', *International Social Work*.

Apt, N.A. and Grieco, M. (1995), *Listening to street girls*, UNICEF, Ghana.

Apt, N.A., Blavo, E. and Opoku, S. (1992), *Street children*, Social Administration Unit, University of Ghana.

Grieco, M., Apt, N. and Turner, J. (1996), *At Christmas and on rainy days: transport, travel and the female traders of Accra*, Avebury: Aldershot.

17 Gender and Access to Education

RIGHT HONOURABLE MADAME DIALLO HADJA AÏCHA BAH
MINISTER OF PRE-UNIVERSITY EDUCATION AND
VOCATIONAL TRAINING, GOVERNMENT OF GUINEA AND
MEMBER OF THE FORUM OF AFRICAN WOMEN IN EDUCATION

Introduction

The year 1996 was declared the Year of Education in Africa by the OAU. That decision clearly illustrates the African governments' realization that in the closing years of the 20th century education remains now more than ever the essential prerequisite for development. This is a major challenge that the continent should take up as quickly as possible, especially the education of girls and women, if it wants to be included among the technologically advanced regions of the world.

Mrs Eddah Gachukia, Director of FAWE, expressed this situation well in other words when, speaking of the implementation of the objectives targeted in the action platform agreed on at the Beijing conference on women's issues, she stated that:

> ... if there has been a problem on which the world has seemed united, this has been the importance of education as an essential instrument for development of human resources and for equipping girls and women so that they may be present in all sectors and levels of development.

The fact is that education of African women is an important key for improving health, nutrition and the cultural level of families and for enabling women to participate in decision-making in society.

One of the basic requirements here is equity in access to education and the establishment of more equal relationships between women and men.

Partnership and networking constitute the most effective strategic approaches in the current context characterized by an unprecedented continent-wide economic crisis which could, if no countermeasures are taken, bring to nought all the efforts made here and there to create the foundations for sustainable development. This partnership involves all the players in the education sector: teachers, local elected officials, lenders and donors, NGOs and the active components of the community.

This is all the more important in that the battle for women's education can only be won through concerted action focusing the energies and inputs of all.

Situation of Guinean women: Some Important Data

Guinean society as a whole is still marked by the phenomenon of reproduction and transmission of certain traditional cultural values which continue to hamper the full sociocultural development of women.

The present situation of Guinean women can be summarized as follows:

a) in relation to education:
- a high illiteracy rate (about 81.16 per cent);
- a low school attendance rate on the part of girls (28.75 per cent);
- a low level of representation of girls and women in technical and vocational education (about 21.1 per cent of all female students);
- the persistence of certain discriminatory sexist stereotypes;

b) in relation to health:
- high maternal mortality rates (623 per 100,00 live births);
- a low rate of contraception (three per cent);
- a marked prevalence of STDs/AIDS (over one per cent);
- persistence of genital mutilation and other practices harmful to women's health;

c) in relation to employment:
- low access to private employment for women (14 per cent);
- absence of any national employment policy favouring women;

d) in relation to access to services:
- credit procedures unsuited to women's needs, resulting in very limited accessibility for women;
- the physically demanding nature of household chores (fetching water, gathering firewood, work in fields, etc.);
- exclusion of women from the benefits of inheritance and land appropriation;

e) in relation to women in difficult situations:
• little assistance for handicapped women;
• double marginalisation of women in difficult circumstances;
• a large percentage of women de facto heads of households (30 per cent in certain regions of the country);
• the weight of sociocultural traditions;
• the poverty that affects women more;

f) in relation to the law and decision-making:
• ignorance of their rights and failure to apply existing laws;
• low representation of women in the decision-making process and in political life (cf. table below).

Table 17.1 Comparative table of numbers of senior women and men officials occupying certain positions of responsibility

No.	Levels of responsibility	Women	Men	Total
1	Ministers/High Commissioners	4	23	27
2	Permanent Secretaries of ministerial departments	4	23	27
3	Principal Private Secretaries of ministerial departments	8	19	27
4	Region governors	0	8	8
5	Prefects	0	33	33
6	Permanent Secretaries of Prefectures	1	65	66
7	Deputies	10	104	114
8	Ambassadors	1	30	31
9	Mayors of communes	3	35	38
	Totals	31	340	371

(i.e. a female representation rate of 8.35 per cent)

In light of these disturbing statistics, numerous initiatives have been developed by the state, the NGOs, the private and associative sector and also other partners, for the promotion of Guinean women. Among these initiatives, the following are worthy of note:

- the creation of a ministry with responsibility for promoting women's and children's interests, whose mandate is to mobilize all the country's synergy in the advancement of women;
- the setting up of numerous women's development organizations (NGOs, associations, group, cooperatives);
- the taking of the 'gender' aspect into account in the national planning process.

The national policy on promotion of women is based on the numerical significance of women, who represent 51 per cent of the country's population. This policy is founded on the following guiding principles:

- gender approach principle in matters of advancement of women, placing the accent on equity in the participation of men and women on an equal footing;
- self-promotion principle based on the struggle against condescending assistance and the assumption of responsibility by women for their own development;
- principle of observance of international commitments concerning promotion of women and compliance with the objectives spelled out by
  1. the World Conference on Education for All (1990)
  2. the World Summit for Children (1990)
  3. the Rio Summit on the Environment and Development (1992)
  4. the World Summit on Human Rights (1993)
  5. the Cairo International Conference on Population and Development (1994)
  6. the World Summit for Social Development (1995)
  7. the fourth World Conference on Women's issues held in Beijing (1995);
- principle of partnership between state, NGOs, civil society and development cooperation agencies in the implementation of the programmes to promote women;
- principle of compliance with national human resource development and population policies.

Finally, it should be stressed that the general objective of this policy is to accelerate the advancement of Guinean women by focusing on reducing the inequalities between men and women and on the efforts to mitigate poverty.

Access of Guinean Girls and Women to Education

The National Basic Education for All Programme undertaken following the Jomtien World Education Conference has set the family as its focus and adopted an integration strategy in favour of girl infants (0–6 years), young girls (7–15 years) and mothers (15–49 years). The aim of this strategy is specifically to improve equity through changes in parents' behaviour concerning education of girls, using reasoning advocating such changes as the primary tool.

The change of behaviour in question will have to be brought about in the minds of the men in particular, since as a study recently made in Guinea on the education of girls in rural areas showed:

> The educated woman has crossed cultural and behavioral frontiers and can therefore no longer act like her sister in the same village who has not experienced this destabilization. For the country people, an educated woman insists on better material living conditions and greater responsibility. For these reasons, they do not consider an educated women will make an ideal wife for a farmer. Accordingly, since marriage is the primary goal for a woman, parents refrain from sending their daughters to school, for fear of compromising their chances of marriage ....

The object is therefore to enable on the one hand development of specific activities through parental education for mothers and future mothers and, on the other hand, to favour increased school attendance and better retention of girls in school.

In the context of the formulation of this document, a small qualitative survey was conducted on the basis of individual interviews and focus groups involving some 30 girls and women ranging in age from 15–27 years.

The sample used consisted of girls and women living in semi-urban areas (Coyah, 50 km from Conakry) and Km 5 in Dubreka (about 45 km from Conakry) and engaged in various occupations (NAFA centre trainees, members of women's groups, fish and seafood merchants, etc.).

The objectives of this survey were two in number:

a) to identify with the interviewees the main hindrances to access to education for them;
b) to determine with them the ways and means best suited for offering them appropriate education services.

The first objective considered in connection with the conditions governing access to education was approached in terms of the following aspects:

- weight of tradition in the lives of rural women;
- amount of time spent on household chores everyday and the considerable physical effort involved (laboriousness);
- position assigned to girls and women by formal schools and the literacy programmes;
- perception of inequity in access to education;
- level of awareness of the women themselves concerning their need to educate themselves and the involvement of the community;
- perception of the purpose of education.

The analysis of the responses regarding these different points shows that the girls and women are aware of the inequity they suffer under because of their social status. On the other hand, however, the rural women seem to accept this state of affairs. This demonstrates to our eyes that their own perception needs to be improved by heightening their awareness and allowing them more responsibility on a permanent basis.

Several interviewees were also of the opinion that they had very little time to devote to their own education, because they are kept busy throughout the day, either supervising and caring for children, preparing the family meal, gardening or a variety of household chores (fetching water, gathering firewood, etc.).

It is clear that this major handicap affecting virtually all rural women can only be resolved by the combined effect of a number of actions:

- involvement of the men in the sharing of household chores;
- easing of the physical labour entailed through utilization of small-scale village technology;
- effective taking into account of the 'gender' approach in the actions designed to arouse awareness concerning education of women by also including their immediate circle, in particular the men (husbands, brothers, fathers, religious leaders, local elected officials, etc.);
- effective integration of women's literacy components in rural development projects and strengthening the possibilities of access to formal education for girls;
- the taking of the beneficiaries' practical needs into consideration when formulating the contents of education and training.

A specific feature noted in the case of girls living in semi-urban areas is that they think of pre-apprenticeship in a trade as the initial personal motivating factor for all training. The case of the pre-vocational training given in the NAFA centres (or second-chance schools) was regularly cited as an example.

With respect to the objective concerning the modalities and conditions of the supply of education, the interviewees most frequently concentrated on the following aspects:

- the necessity of offering education contents closely linked with either access to a vocational opening (case of girls in semi-urban areas), or else improvement of their living and working conditions (functional literacy for rural women);
- the necessity of providing material and financial support for associations, groups and members of women's NGOs with a view to facilitating easing of their daily work;
- organizing training actions centred around income-generating activities for the women concerned.

Among the important conclusions drawn from this small survey, mention should first be made of the fact that the girls and women surveyed are fully aware that they have an education deficiency that works to their disadvantage. They accordingly evidence considerable interest in any education opportunity offered that will not 'disrupt' their activities.

Then secondly, it must be borne in mind that the primary motivation most frequently cited by the interviewees is that they are all the more favourably inclined toward any form of education or training if it will enable them to improve their earning capacity and help them to take better care of their families. These two findings are important in that they should serve as guidance for any approach to formulating an education strategy, taking into account the needs and expectations of the beneficiaries.

Role of the Partners: Regional and Local Networking

At National Level

In accordance with the government's political will and the recommendations of the different specialised international conferences, convergent multisectoral strategies have been initiated at the central, regional and local levels in order to create the material and psychological foundations that will facilitate education for women. These comprise measures developed by the state, the NGOs and certain donors, and include:

Actions carried out by the state Several governmental institutions are involved in the education of girls and women in Guinea. The following can be cited by way of examples:

- the National Literacy Service, which is making very significant efforts in the non-formal sector in complementation of those conducted in the formal sector, through the Education Sector Adjustment Programme (PASE), by the Pre-University Education Department. In 1996 this service launched an important programme entitled 'Women for Woman' in the literacy centres, which aims at having the better educated and trained women serve as tutors for those who are less educated:
- the National Basic Education for All Commission (CONEBAT), institutionalised to support the follow-up of the Jomtien recommendations, is the main agency concerned with the establishment at national level of NAFA centres, with UNICEF support. These centres have attracted 4,201 young people aged between 9 and 16 years, some of whom have participated in formal education and some not, 80 per cent of them being girls, and who have been placed in a school-type learning situation;
- the National Agricultural Extension Programme (PNVA) which instructs women's groups and associations, training them in certain improved farming techniques;
- the Expanded Programme on Immunization (EPI/PHC/ED) is developing sub-programmes aimed particularly at rural areas in the fields of health education, sanitation, family planning and responsible parenthood;
- the National Directorate for the Advancement of Women carries out an important group of education actions in the Support Centres for Self-Promotion of Women (CAAF) set up at prefecture level. These CAAFs seek to organize women's work better, to train girls for learning trades and to support income-generating activities.

Actions carried out by the NGOs Several dozens of NGOs specialized in education are working at the regional and peripheral levels in particular to promote specific actions benefiting women.

Some of them are solely concerned with education, through functional literacy (OVODEC/AGEED), others play an advocate role (FAWE, Guinea branch) and yet others are involved in awareness arousal and combating practices harmful to women (COFEG, ASFEGMASSI, CPETAFE, etc.).

At African Level

To complement the initiatives developed at country level, federative-type approaches are under way and must be strengthened. These include in particular the expansion and strengthening of FAWE's actions at national (national branches), sub-regional and regional (networking) levels to foster larger- scale arousal of public awareness and encourage the emergence of new behaviours favourable to sustainable education of girls and women (coordination of the NGOs' work).

To this end, synergy-promoting and complementary approaches must be instituted at the national, sub-regional and regional levels through effective application of the recommendations of the Cairo and Beijing international conferences, especially as regards the gender approach and the plea.

The main architect of this approach at continent level will unquestionably be FAWE (Forum of African Women in Education), a unique organization of women who are education ministers, university vice-chancellors and leading decision-makers engaged in the promotion of education for girls and women through policies and practices to that end.

Through both its headquarters in Nairobi (Kenya) and its 40 or so members spread over 26 African countries, FAWE will play a vanguard role in the coordination and facilitation of implementation of the education component of the world action platform in favour of women.

To do so, FAWE will have to strengthen the work of its national branches, develop a partnership with the other parties involved (NGOs, lenders and donors, media, communities) and maximize the impact of the regional approaches in a perfect synergy.

These synergy-enhanced approaches will favour the formulation and implementing of an Education Agenda for Africa that meets women's concerns.

Based on the survey referred to above, the women's recommendations as to this agenda centre around the following ideas:

• strengthening of the activities performed by FAWE and other competent organizations as regards presenting the case and arousing public opinion in favour of education for women. This action will have to be carried out in concrete terms through recourse to community opinion leaders and other persuaders, with a view to increasing community support and securing

more dynamic backing from education personnel and institutions;
- contribution to the setting up, through FAWE sub-regional and national branches, of measures that will encourage the placing and retention of girls in school (scholarships, appropriate training courses, access to trades);
- intensification of the reproduction of models of successful women in Africa through the media and school texts (historical figures, successful women entrepreneurs, etc.).

At National Level

- Development of girls schools in the formal system. Linking of income-generating activities to functional literacy programmes.
- Large-scale awareness arousal among men by means of rural radio regarding education for girls and women.
- Elimination of discriminatory stereotypes of girls from school programmes and texts.
- Establishment of schools and training centres close to where women live and work.
- Taking women's vocational concerns into account in the contents of education programmes.
- Improvement of the image of women teachers. Strengthening of community participation and of the support provided by NGOs and donors for school construction.
- Establishment of a fruitful and permanent teacher-parent dialogue to favour effective assumption by the community of responsibility for dealing with school attendance problems.
- Using all available means to combat the causes of girls dropping out of school.

Abbreviations

AGEED	Association Guinéenne pour l'enseignement et l'éducation pour le Développement [Guinean Association for Education for Development]
ASFEGMASSI	Association des Femmes Guinéennes pour la lutte contre les maladies sexuellement transmissibles et le SIDA [Association of Guinean Women for Combating Sexually Transmitted Diseases and AIDS]
CAAF	Centre d'Appui à l'Auto-promotion Féminine [Support Centre for Self-Promotion of Women]
COFEG	Coordination des ONG féminines de Guinée [Coordinating Organization for Guinean Women's NGOs]
CONEBAT	Commission Nationale d'Education de Base pour Tous [National Basic Education for All Commission]
CPETAFE	Cellule de lutte contre les practiques traditionnelles néfastes à la santé de la femme et de l'enfant [Group for Combating Traditional Practices Harmful to the Health of Women and Children]
UEPI/PHC/ED	Expanded Programme on Immunization/Primary Health Care/Essential Drugs
FAWE	Forum of African Women in Education
NGO	Non-governmental organization
OAU	Organization of African Unity
OVODEC	Organisation des Volontaires pour le Développement de l'Education et de la Culture [Organization of Volunteers for the Development of Education and Culture]
PASE	Programme d'Ajustement Sectoriel de l'Education [Education Sector Adjustment Programme]
PNVA	Programme National de Vulgarisation Agricole [National Agricultural Extension Programme]
STD	Sexually transmitted diseases

PART 3
CONNECTING UP WITH THE RESOURCES – A GUIDE TO DONOR FUNDING

PART 3

18 On-line Development Resources: Accessing Donors' Gender Capabilities

MARGARET GRIECO
PROFESSOR OF ORGANISATION AND DEVELOPMENT
MANAGEMENT, UNIVERSITY OF NORTH LONDON AND
PROFESSOR NANA ARABA APT, DIRECTOR, CENTRE FOR
SOCIAL POLICY STUDIES, UNIVERSITY OF GHANA

Introduction: On-line Donor Development

Donors show a growing awareness of the potential of new information technologies for improving their development practice. Many donors have increased transparency around their development operations by establishing web sites which give up to date information on organisational goals, projects, programmes and budgets. For example, the British Department for International Development (DFID) under the leadership of a cabinet minister, the Right Honourable Clare Short, operates a web site which offers a rapid overview of the organisation of British development aid.

For African women's organisations seeking to ensure that aid is better targeted towards women's needs, knowledge of and access to such sites is imperative. Scrutiny of the White Paper available on the DFID web site, for example, reveals that, whilst the detail of the paper recognises the importance of gender issues in Africa, gender is not explicitly mentioned in any of the 12 headings which set out the 'strands' for action. The failure to headline gender in such an important document may very well have its consequences for the development and achievement of the type of gender policies and goals sought after by African women in the African Platform for Action and in the Beijing Platform for Action. However, on the same web site but in different documents 'progress towards gender equity and the empowerment of women' are heralded as key components of Britain's development aid policies.

Clearly, there is an active role for African women to play in ensuring a transparent and consistent development policy on the part of donors. The

207

DFID web site stresses the importance of involving and cooperating with voluntary organisations in development aid: it does not, however, stress the importance of involving women's organisations in its new approach to development. Through connecting up with the web site, African women's organisations can identify the gaps in the British vision of development aid in respect of gender and feedback to the development agencies as researchers, operational agencies and beneficiaries. Presently, the DFID site, as with many of the donor sites, does not have a provision for electronic client feedback into the site or the minister's office. Interestingly, this British site has no discussion of the connectivity needs of Africa's women's organisations – interestingly because the British government has already launched electronic consultation on the next Budget and upon the Freedom of Information Act, ground breaking innovations in terms of electronic democracy.

In addition to possessing their own web sites which give information on their own organisational activities, budgets and mission statements or organisational goals, donors have entered the business of creating electronic fora on which 'brainstorming' and electronic debate around problems, solutions and innovations relevant to development take place. A good example of such a forum and one which is still on line, although the implementation recommendations of the forum have still to be rendered concrete by the sponsors, is the Global Knowledge 97 initiative. Sponsored and championed by the Canadian government, a pioneer in its search to ensure equitable access to electronic communications, and the World Bank, an organisation which under the leadership of its president James Wolfensohn is committed to improving connectivity within the developing world, Global Knowledge 97 paralleled its physical conference on knowledge management with a virtual conference. This virtual conference has enabled the voices of organisations and individuals in the developing world to be heard, with African discussants playing a very active part in placing their concerns and ideas on the agenda in this new form of consultation. Encouraging donors and professional organisations to set up parallel virtual conferences (and technical facilities to support those virtual conferences in locations in developing countries) is an important step in enhancing the opportunities for African women to raise their voices in the development discourse: virtual attendance may often be more possible for women who are typically time poor than physical attendance at distant locations.

Although the development of donor web sites and virtual conferences provide a means in theory for women's organisations to more readily collect information with which to shape their lobbying strategies and venues at which they can articulate the importance of their participation in the development agenda, unless moves are made towards improving the connectivity of women's organisations then women will suffer once more the traditional resource disadvantages of their gender: technology will be operated and owned by the men. However, there are organisations which have begun to focus on the importance of improving connectivities in rural areas, such as the Dutch NGO TOOL along with VITA (Volunteers in Technical Assistance which is about to launch an innovative scheme for bringing connectivity to rural Africa. Such improvements which may very well benefit rural women. African women explicitly and repeatedly ask for improvements in their connectivity: donors could do much to facilitate the improvement.

Supplying development information on the World Wide Web implies a commitment to ensuring that those most affected by this information can access it and key donor agencies have begun to pay attention to the need to develop African connectivity. A pioneer programme in this respect has been the UNDP Sustainable Development Networking Programme. This programme, launched in 1992, views information and communication technologies (ICT) as a major tool to foster decentralised, informed, participatory, effective governance at all levels of society and in the developing world. 35 countries have SDNP projects. The Programme is explicitly concerned with ensuring that the global information society can benefit the poor, community-based organisations and business. The SDNP has a very useful web site: scrutiny of the web site indicates that gender receives minimal consideration despite the predominance of women amongst the world's poor and the voluble demands from African women for gender equitable access to connectivity.

There are a number of other important donor initiatives concerned to provide connectivity for Africa and which provide potential channels for the voices of African Women. The Canadian International Development Agency, CIDA, has set up the South African Legislative Virtual Conferencing Project which links nine provincial legislatures of South Africa with their provincial counterparts in Canada for the exchange of information, skills and expertise. USAID, an organisation which operates a high quality web site, has set up the Leland project which seeks to provide connectivity for 20 African countries.

The discussion of gender issues in connectivity upon the various web sites of the international donors is sparse. An exception is to be found on the Finnish Aid web site.

(Text taken from the Finnish Aid web site) During their first months online, Kenyans have obtained much important information on what causes underdevelopment and how to defeat it, Ngola (a local informant) explains. 'It has helped the dissemination of information pertaining to development issues including (the) women conference in [Beijing].'

This site which is yet in the early stages of development is seeking to draw attention to the connectivity opportunities and needs of Africa and in its discussion of connectivity in Namibia, it draws attention to gender equity issues in access to information communication technology. As of yet, the gender and connectivity issue has not received explicit funding – or if it has such funding is not displayed on the home page – but the page invites user feedback and provides a bulletin board upon which African women can place their voices in the request for a fairer share of communication space and resources. Another exception is to be found at the Global Knowledge 97 meeting and corresponding web site, sponsored by the Canadian International Development Agency and the World Bank, where concern with gender issues in connectivity is explicit. At the physical meeting, over 30 per cent of the delegates were women. Leadership on the connectivity issue was given by James Wolfensohn, President of the World Bank:

> 'If you look around the world, you'll see that women are development,' said James Wolfensohn, the president of the World Bank to a thousand people attending a breakfast forum. 'The arrival of information technology in terms of education for women is the breakthrough we've been waiting for,' he said (quotation taken from the CIDA web site).

Finally, there are NGO and private sector web sites which are ready to host materials generated by African women in the bid to raise their concerns more effectively, publicly and transparently within the development discourse. AVIVA operate a women's issues web site which will host material from African women (http://www.aviva.org), the Norwegian Council for Africa (http://www.fellesraadet.africainfo.no) operates a high quality Internet directory service on Africa and African issues. As African web sites develop, these sites may find it useful to encourage donors like the Bank, USAID and the other donors to include these sites on the list of links provided by these international agencies. This will increase the visibility of these African sites: similarly, African organisations, especially women's organisations may find it useful to lobby for some space within donor home pages themselves.

The field is developing rapidly and what looked as if it was impossible when the UNSDNP initiative was launched has already began to happen. The purpose of this chapter is to give some indication of the extent to which the development discourse has already moved into electronic form and to sketch the ways in which these developments can assist African women in the bid for an equitable share of development resources, development participation and development vision.

The rest of this chapter reviews various development donor web sites with the intention of assisting those African women new to this way of making contact with development agencies to enter the electronic development forum and bid more effectively for resources, both local and global.

Canadian International Development Agency

URL (web address): http://www.acdi-cida.gc.ca/

This site is well organised in terms of accessing materials on gender. It has an open search function which enables the user to immediately access gender materials including overviews of agency policy on gender, specific gender projects and programmes. This organisation of the web site reflects the emphasis given to gender within Canadian development policy – gender is one of the six headline themes.

The site provides facilities for electronic public consultation on country programme reviews – these facilities potentially enable women's organisations to communicate their views on programmes directly to the organisation. In this sense, the site is interactive, however, one user can not access the views of another user on the country programme – only the development agency has sight of the feedback. This form of feedback does not amount to a forum but it is a solid beginning.

The site has electronic forms and check lists for internships – this format could be extended and adopted for, for example, developing country women's groups applications for resources. At present, the electronic application format is set up to serve Canadian interests rather than developing partner needs.

The site is friendly to users of machines with slow connections. No extra programmes are needed to access detailed materials on the site.

At present, the organisational information provided does not assist women's groups in locating officers with responsibility for gender within the organisation. More precise contact information is required in order to assist development partners articulate their needs and transmit their knowledge.

The site has a full array of gender materials which could usefully be downloaded for advocacy, operational, research and teaching purposes. The site could usefully organise some of these materials into a 'topic package' format so that users in developing countries can use these for distant education purposes.

Department for International Development (United Kingdom)

URL (web address): http://www.oneworld.org/oda

This site is not well organised in terms of accessing information on gender activities in Africa or in terms of outlining programmes under which African women's organisations can bid for resources. The site has, however, great potential to be better organised in these respects as its primary commitment is to poverty alleviation and within its own materials it recognises that 70 per cent of the world's poor are composed of women.

Identifying designated personnel concerned with gender issues and giving electronic contact information for such personnel would represent a good first start.

The site carries current and useful policy materials such as ministerial speeches, White Paper on Development, development budget statistics.

The site is not organised to enable users to access details on specific projects.

The site is not interactive except in respect of ordering materials and documents from the information service.

European Commission, DG VII

URL (web address): http://europa.eu.int/en/comm/dg08/dgvii.htm

This site identifies gender development as a policy of the European Union development agency, DG VII. However, the site contains no explicit materials on gender other than this statement. The site has no search function to allow the easy identification of projects which may have a gender component.

The site enables the user to identify projects by country although this facility has primarily been set up in order to permit commercial agencies to identify commercial opportunities in development.

The site enables the user to identify desk officers for the various developing countries and gives contact information for these officers, although no electronic contact facility has been set up within the system.

The site is available in a number of languages.

The site is not interactive and provides no facilities for electronic consultation or feedback.

Finnaid: Department for International Development and Cooperation

URL (web address): http://virtual.finland.fi

This web site is still under development, however, it has begun by inviting users to provide material for inclusion in its section on how to make use of the new information communication technologies to help the poor. It has an emergent section on Internet connections and grassroot experience of the Internet which could be used by African women to amplify their voices.

The site does not have a search function but is still so small that this is not yet a problem.

The site does not give access to information on specific gender projects nor does it identify gender personnel or contact numbers for those wishing to gain information on gender issues.

The site contains a section on non-governmental organisations and the intention of the agency to make use of NGO partnership in development operations, however, the site is sparse on information. Given the invitation of the donor to users for feedback, African women organisations could provide materials with which to expand upon this section.

UNDP Sustainable Development Networking Programme

URL (web address): http://www3.undp.org/

This web site provides an excellent portrayal of an operational and pioneer connectivity programme.

The user can get down through the regional level to the national level operations.

The materials on the rationale for connectivity in developing countries and the mechanisms for implementing the programme are well organised and easily accessible by users; however, there is no search function by which issues such as gender can easily be accessed.

The site contains very little on the importance of the gender and connectivity issue. African women organisations could profitably lobby for a greater level of inclusion in this programme.

United Nations

URL (web address): http://www.un.org

This site contains a wealth of materials useful to women's organisations interested in participating in development policy.

The site provides good guidance on how to make contact with the various departments of the UN organisational structure, providing good electronic contact link ups with the personnel specified as having responsibility for particular areas.

Accessing and downloading UN reports is a relatively simple business and these materials can help local experts and consultants build up locally available data bases in a context where current reports and materials are often difficult to access.

USAID, the United States Agency for International Development

URL (web address): http://www.info.usaid.gov/

This site has no open search function which permits the ready location of gender materials.

The site has provision for materials under a headline 'Gender and Participation': however, at the time of writing the link is not working.

The site does carry gender materials on particular initiatives such as the Women's Political Participation and Legal Rights Initiative set up by Madelaine Albright as a US contribution to Beijing, but these take diligent searching to access.

In its discussion of NGO capacity-building the site does make explicit mention of the need to harness the capacity of women's organisations. Once again, it takes diligent searching to access the materials.

The site contains an abundance of useful development materials: however, the site is not well set up for users in developing countries who may have slow connections. Accessing documents frequently requires the downloading and installation of additional programmes – a situation which creates difficulties at the developing countries end.

The site has a useful set of links to other donor agencies and development web sites – some of these are dated and no longer function but the majority seem to be functional.

The World Bank

URL (web address): http://www.worldbank.org

This site is currently under considerable redevelopment: however, at present it is not well organised in terms of accessing information on gender. Although the site has a facility for open searching by the simple entry of a key word, in the case of 'gender' this does not link back to the central gender home page of the Bank but links only to the materials of the Africa region (there is a link through the Africa region to the central gender home page but it is at the time of writing defective). In order to reach the central gender home page of the Bank, the user has to click onto 'Topics in Development', then click onto 'Human Resources and Poverty' and then click onto 'Poverty and Social Policy' and then click onto 'Gender' – under this arrangement 'gender' is virtually buried in terms of a novice outsider trying to connect up with the Bank resources.

The site has a number of useful gender resources including agricultural tool kits, best practice information, contact information on persons responsible for gender within the Bank organisational structure: however, as the site stands, it provides neither a good overview of aggregate gender activities within the Bank nor an easy tracking system on gender projects or gender components within projects conducted by the institution.

The contact information on Bank officers with a responsibility for gender is in effect an embryonic electronic client feedback system – outsiders can connect up with Bank officers through email: however, there is no coordinated system for tracking client feedback.

This site has an electronic gender journal which has real potential as a mechanism through which African women can raise their voices.

Global Knowledge 97

URL (web address) http://www.globalknowledge.org

This site provides a facility for placing ideas and development requests on a high visibility communication channel. The recommendations made on the site are visible not only to the sponsors (the Canadian government and the World Bank) but are also visible to other organisations in the development community. Whilst there has been no reported take up of ideas by either of the sponsors as of yet, there has been a lot of contact between other agencies and organisations off-line (based upon their postings on line) resulting in the setting up of new initiatives such as workshops to align poverty alleviation and equitable access to connectivity.

Recommendations

There are a number of simple steps that most development aid agencies could take to make their web sites more gender friendly and amenable to African women's organisations searching for technical information on gender issues and attempting to identify relevant contact points within organisations for potential partnerships in the field of development. These are:

- provide a (working) 'gender' search function within the web site;
- provide an organisational chart of staff with responsibility for gender within the organisation plus contact information;
- provide an overview of the gender activities within the organisation and a listing of gender projects or projects with gender components and the officers responsible for those projects;
- provide an electronic feedback mechanism which is transparent to all users of the web site (an independent moderator can be used to ensure that abusive materials do not get conveyed on the system) so that senior personnel and external agencies such as women's organisations can both access this flow of information on development problems, successes and opportunities;
- provide application forms for participation in partnership programmes, development funds and research funds on the web site. These can be downloaded and completed in conventional fashion or completed electronically, it will however enable women's organisations to overcome the well known vagaries of the postal services;

- provide hypertext links to related sites. This assists organisations in developing countries to locate important information at reduced search costs;
- pay attention in the design and format of web sites to the needs of users with slow connections;
- the major donors should set up a forum to consider the most effective ways of laying out web sites in order to service the needs of grassroots organisations, most particularly women.

African women's organisations could usefully take the following steps:

- make use of existing donor web sites for amplifying their voices in the call for proper gender representation in the development discourse;
- provide donors with feedback on how to make their web sites more gender friendly;
- lobby for improvements of the connectivity of African women;
- develop African gender web sites and organise 'advertisement' of these web sites on donor home pages;
- use the Internet as a way of collecting funding independently through linkage with major credit organisations such as Visa card;
- develop a new form gender agenda which makes good use of the communication revolution – for example, harness new intelligent communication in micro-credit and micro-banking.

The existence of new on-line communication technologies necessitates the skilling of African women in these new technologies if they are to take their proper place in the development debate; Abantu, a Canadian NGO has just set up such a training scheme in East Africa. The demand for these skills is clearly there – the organisation of development assistance must be shaped to satisfy it.

19 New Technology, New Horizons: The Prospect of More Client-focused Development Banking

MARGARET GRIECO
PROFESSOR OF ORGANISATION AND DEVELOPMENT
MANAGEMENT, UNIVERSITY OF NORTH LONDON AND
STEPHEN DENNING, DIRECTOR OF KNOWLEDGE
MANAGEMENT, WORLD BANK

Introduction: The Drive to Connect

In Africa, the need to improve the effectiveness of the development process is urgent: a lengthy period of financial support and external technical assistance has produced mixed results. In surveys undertaken by some development agencies, clients perceive that the authority for substantial action on the part of the development institutions is still retained by the managers and staff within those institutions. The distance between the field and headquarters produces multiple and complex levels of red tape and plentiful instances of crossed messages and inefficiency.

The internal processes of the institutional aid and development agencies are often obscure from the perspective of African clients. While the development agencies increasingly require transparency in the procedures and processes of their African clients, there is also a need to enhance transparency in the development agencies themselves. For African clients, tracking the status of the funding of a programme, project or even workshop within the international agencies is often no easy business. Telephone contacts are frequently unfruitful. Faxes go missing in vast bureaucracies. What is easily established within the communications environment in a single developed country in America, Europe or Japan is a nightmare in the African context: different time zones, rationing of communications access, overloaded systems and faulty technologies, can make chasing down a headquarters project officer a tedious and frustrating ordeal. Frequently, the internal organisation of aid and development agencies means that their local offices are not able, or are not always motivated to assist the client in his or her search for the relevant personnel. Frequent changes of staff assignments and reorganisations within the international institutions tend to tear apart the personal networks that can sometimes avoid or circumvent bureaucratic difficulties. And there are the fundamental asymmetries in the system: the development agency can afford to transport headquarters personnel to the field at will, or transport clients to headquarters with ease, but the client often lacks the resources for headquarters to button down an agreement that has slipped or is in danger of slipping.

What can be done about the present state of intercontinental development action? Two obvious steps are increasingly being taken. First, development agencies can place personnel with high levels of authority in the field. In this way, clients have the requisite access to ensure that their case, their objectives, their problems receive adequate attention. Many bilateral agencies are already organised in this manner and some of the international agencies are moving in this direction.

Second, the communications technology between headquarters and Africa can be improved. Some of this improvement is a matter of investing in infrastructure, and indeed some donors such as the World Bank and USAID are presently involved in financing the expansion of Internet facilities in African countries, as well as helping African countries break up state telecommunications monopolies that constrain private sector financing. Importantly, some of the needed improvement is a matter of reorganising development agency communications systems and protocols, so that they can better connect with their clients and their clients can more easily connect with them. Electronic client feedback can be both cheap and efficient when properly organised: and it can be readily directed to or accessed by senior management rendering the problems experienced by clients (and the blockages in the system) more transparent at the top levels of the organisation.

When designing or redesigning the communication systems for development agencies, institutions have to consider explicitly how to enable their clients to operate within this architecture (Cerny, 1966; Armstrong and Hagel, 1996). In the world of manufacturing, leading companies have already developed communication arrangements which allow clients to interface electronically with the interior administrative structure of the factory. In a recent article in the *Harvard Business Review* of July/August 1996, Upton and McAfee described the operation of McDonnel Douglas' Missouri factory under the banner 'the real virtual factory'. McDonnel Douglas have had the communications structure of this factory designed so that the clients and other business partners can interface electronically with the operations of the plant. There are 400 internal and external members of the communications network, a membership which includes both long-term and more casual partners. Conducting business within this virtual framework is both more convenient and time-efficient; on-line interaction also has the benefit of allowing clients greater possibilities in customising their orders (Burke, 1996). New technology opens the possibilities of the levels of interaction and iteration between organisations and clients necessary for the ready customizing of products. In carpet production, customers can through computer-aided design produce the good they want on-screen and transmit it to a factory where it is manufactured.

Virtual manufacturing and virtual organization are already with us: the linking of client and services over distance is already a reality (Grieco and Jones, 1994). And given the spatial structures of development banking, it is a model which could and should be readily adopted by development banking. Within a virtual framework, clients are better able to track the current status of their business within a distant organisation and are enabled to have sufficiently frequent and rapid interaction to refine the shape of the goods they purchase. Clients in development banking, given the spatial and cultural distances involved, can be viewed as being in specific need of such facilities.

How possible is it to accommodate development clients with varying levels of information/technology sophistication? In the case of McDonnel Douglas, the communications system was designed so as to accommodate network members whose information/technology sophistication varied enormously. Designing a system of virtual development banking would most certainly involve a substantial accommodation of variations in the range of information/ technology sophistication of network members, but as the McDonnel Douglas example demonstrates, and the growing international assistance for connectivity in developing countries indicates, there are solutions to such problems.

It is clear there is a sound rationale for the development of Internet connections between Africa and donors; similarly, it is clear that some donors have begun to invest in the infrastructure. But do the clients want it? There has been no Africa-wide survey on the topic, but certain client groups have already spoken.

At Beijing, African women pushed for the development and provision of network technologies which would let them better connect, one with another, and with the outside world. In particular, the request was for access to email. Indeed, the argument was given in a graphic form with one of the Beijing cartoons showing a line of African women head-loading lap-top computers upon which they typed as they walked.

At a recent post-Beijing meeting of African women in Africa (Voices from African Women, 1996), the request for better communication technologies to link African women's organisations one with another and with the outside world was repeated. In one recent workshop organised by an international donor to gauge African priorities for assistance, African participants put Internet connectivity as a very high priority.

On the ground, the Internet has already begun to have its impact in Africa. For instance, in June 1995, a health worker in the remote town of Kamana in Zambia sought and obtained the answer to a question on how to treat malaria from the World Wide Web site of the Center for Disease Control (CDC) in Atlanta, USA (http://www.cdc.com). Many aspects of the occurrence are striking. It took place June 1995, not June 2015. This took place not in the capital of Zambia, but in Kamana, some 600 kilometres from the capital. It took place not in a rich country, or even a middle-income country, but in one of the poorer countries of the world. And it took place in Africa, not in a region where the Internet is well established.

In both Kenya and Ghana, locally developed home pages and World Wide Web sites are already in place. The commercial sector in Ghana has already begun to develop Internet cafés, a development which will greatly enlarge public access to the Internet and modern communication channels. Such commercial facilities have great potential as gateways for communication between development clients and development agency headquarters and indeed, local development offices as well.

However, not all the clients of Africa are eager for high technology networks which erase many of the conventional difficulties posed by gaining good service over distance. Certain governments are strongly resistant to the establishment of Internet and email facilities within their national space (Spar and Bussgang, 1996) – one such case has been the government of Ethiopia, a particularly significant case as both the United Nations Economic Commission for Africa and the Organisation for African Unity headquarters are located in Addis Ababa. Such problems are unlikely to prove permanent, as the global movement towards openness and connectivity hurtles forward. But African countries – already behind in many domains of development – could lose precious time and fall even further behind in the race for competitiveness if these blockages are not removed quickly. Moreover the opportunities to leapfrog countries and organisations with an antiquated legacy of computer and communications systems in need of expensive updating may be lost.

Equally, not all the managers and staff of development agencies are eager to enter a world of electronic communication and open sharing of information and knowledge. Part of this hesitancy relates to a continuing discomfort with modern communication technology: one manager in one bilateral agency estimates that less than half of the staff of the agency are ready for the transition. Part of it reflects a clinging to a culture of information hoarding: the open sharing of knowledge requires a change in mind-sets for many that are accustomed to, and comfortable in, a hierarchical organisational structure in which control of information is one of the key levers of power. Upgrading the skills of staff in the development agencies and engineering the necessary organisational culture shift will be a large task, but an essential one, if development assistance is to play a useful role in the 21st century. New technologies and new approaches in communications thus provide a key opportunity for incorporating direct client feedback into the very structure and processes of development organisations, permitting the establishment of better services that meet the true objectives and needs of the clients.

In this introduction, we have identified recent client demands and donor moves for high technology connections between Africa and donors and provided a preliminary exploration of the benefits of such a connection. The rest of this chapter will look at the potential benefits of virtual development banking for both client and donor organisations.

Keeping on Course: The Benefits of Direct Client Feedback

There are then new technical possibilities for direct interaction between development banking clients and development agency headquarters. To date, much of the discussion around linking Africa with the new communications technologies has focused on increasing Africa's access to knowledge held elsewhere. However, the need to receive information out of Africa and to incorporate African expert knowledge and beneficiary experience in development project and programme design is every bit as vital (Schein, 1996). Currently, client feedback is obtained – where it is obtained at all – through expensive stand-alone surveys: even more direct and prompt feedback could be more routinely obtained and in a more readily customised fashion through the use of new technologies. Integrating client feedback channels into the core communications systems of development agencies is crucial. The reduced costs of these arrangements and the heightened ability that this provides for the fine tuning of development projects, and thus for project success, make their inclusion in the communication system architecture of the development agencies a matter of priority.

A key benefit of integrating client feedback channels and opportunities into the communications system architecture of the development agency is that it permits clients and beneficiaries to initiate actions for the design and redesign of better projects. Designing projects is inherently an iterative process. The new communications technology, when combined with a greater openness and receptiveness to client viewpoints, could greatly accelerate the process of design improvement.

Current client feedback survey methodologies depend on meeting agendas set outside of the clients' context and environment. With the new technologies and communications approaches, clients can 'talk' to one another about their experiences on electronic bulletin boards and in other electronic fora, prior to tabling points for action in their exchange with the development agency (Robertson et al., 1996). The emerging idea of an electronic 'town hall meeting' is of pivotal importance not only for better governance, but also for better development assistance and development banking. At the heart of this vision is the recognition that new technology opens up possibilities for the direct registration of preferences to an extent and at a frequency never previously experienced. The technology provides in effect the first-ever opportunity for large-scale direct democracy.

Electronic communication channels not only provide clients with the opportunity to register their preferences and to indicate their difficulties with current arrangements but they also provide clients with opportunities to monitor and track the performance of the development institutions. Better quality access to information on the performance of development institution provides clients with the capability of providing better quality feedback to development agencies on these same processes. With present supervision and feedback methods and approaches, news about design flaws and implementation problems can take years to reach key decision-makers with the force and clarity needed to elicit changes in project design. The new technologies and communications approaches could shorten this process to months or even days.

Direct client feedback could clearly assist in getting development projects and programmes on track – and keeping them on track – but how can the communication systems architectures of the development agencies be developed so as to support it? While in the majority of the local offices of development agencies in Africa, development workers enjoy high technology and high quality modes of communication with head offices, the majority of clients and beneficiaries in the surrounding environment often have no such access. To overcome this constraint, development agencies could dedicate working spaces in their local offices where local clients and beneficiaries could access headquarters. Gateway facilities could be designed which provided local clients and beneficiaries with email accounts within a dedicated network in order to pursue their business with headquarters in situations where such business is not local office business, or cannot be pursued satisfactorily with the local office. Similarly, development agencies could make such facilities available through using the services of commercial agencies such as the Internet cafés of Ghana.

However for these electronic gateways to development agency headquarters to work efficiently, development agencies have to redesign their existing internal communication processes – most particularly the ease with which the progress of any item of business can be tracked electronically within the interior of the organisation. The move towards increasing use of electronic information systems in most agencies should make electronic tracking of business a real possibility in the not-too-distant future, provided that it is accompanied by a willingness to share information. But even with such internal transparency within organisations, external clients may need assistance in identifying where in the organisation their communications should be aimed; and the development organisation itself requires information on how quickly client feedback and client requests are dealt with. In the McDonnel Douglas system, there is a 'broker' performing similar types of functions. The establishment of electronic gateways may very well necessitate the emergence of such a broker function within development agencies.

To ensure that client gateways have their full impact on senior management awareness of the blockages and opportunities of the development process, opening up email accounts which have the specific purpose of encouraging clients to feedback to the top of the organisation is crucial. Frequently, senior management intention to expand the development discourse so as to better include clients is frustrated by the territorial behaviours and exclusionary gate-keeping of lower level officers of development organisations. Special direct email lines to senior management open to any client or beneficiary could help ensure that messages do not disappear within the system. The model and rationale for development of an open line for client feedback to management is already present – such lines are already in existence within development agencies: direct messages from clients to managers are less likely to be distorted or suppressed than those transmitted through the traditional hierarchical process of bureaucracy (Ferlie and Pettigrew, 1996) The appointment of staff dedicated full-time to analysing and disseminating key findings from such feedback could also help ensure that development agencies not only go through the motions of listening, but also actually act on the feedback they receive. The linking of personnel evaluation systems for managers to client feedback has proven to be a powerful catalyst in the private sector, and may well be a necessary ingredient for ensuring truly client-oriented development organisations.

Accessing the Micro-environment, Expanding the Client Range: The Potential of the New Technologies

So far we have concentrated on what new technologies can do to improve the experience of the present range of development banking clients. New technology allows both client and senior manager to be in more immediate contact with one another and so keep the development project programme on track. But new technology has an important potential which we have not so far discussed: new technology provides the opportunity for development bankers to go beyond their conventional 'macro' clients in African governments, particularly in ministries of finance and planning. Historically, lending to micro-clients such as village organisations and women's groups was a complex and risky activity for institutions such as development banks which were located great geographical distances from the field. As a consequence, lending to the grassroots happened primarily by routing any assistance through governments. Governments would borrow in order to finance grassroots activity: they would be the development banking client and channel resources down to the grassroots through their own administrative mechanisms.

This mode of financing grassroots development activities has had mixed results and has increasingly come under criticism, not least from the grassroots. There are many factors responsible for the mixed results, but one of them was the use of ineffective communications. Controlling or even monitoring complex sets of financial interactions over distance through a people-based reporting system or bureaucratic hierarchy worked against moving operations in the direction of micro-activities, and correspondingly created the space for abuses of the system, including divergence of resources for non-project purposes.

New technology, particularly if accompanied by a new openness to communicate, offers the opportunity to move development banking in directions that are more responsive to micro-needs, as well as curtail the divergence of resources for non-project purposes. Reducing the number of people-based approvals and information-transfers been organisation and project reduces the number of brokerage points where rents can be extracted.

An example of such a process can be found in the Indian railway system where getting ready access to a ticket frequently involved the payment of a small 'brokerage' fee to the railway clerk selling the ticket. The advent of automatic ticket machines reduced the brokerage space and limited the possibility of ticket clerks charging the passengers rents.

Similarly, with conventional banking in developing countries: bank clerks frequently require 'dash' from customers in order to process their business. Automatic banking facilities could reduce the space for extracting a rent.

So with development banking, establishing electronic channels through which clients can apply for services and through which the development bank can monitor the client's repayment performance over a distance could simultaneously reduce the number of points at which 'rent' can be extracted and expand the size of the micro-customer base available to development banking. The speed and directness of communication could have the benefit of generating a more appropriate portfolio of sustainable development projects.

This vision is not far-fetched: the Grameen Bank has recently taken the new information communication technologies into the field in Bangladesh. Women's groups now have access to the new home banking technologies and development bankers have just gained increased transparency at low cost over microfinanced projects. The old adage that 'it takes $1,000 to place $1 for development in the field' need no longer be true. There is now a choice where information technology can make microfinance the appropriate, sustainable and transparent development banking option.

Clearly, the emergence of development home banking requires the simultaneous fostering of complementary technologies and procedures. Taking the technology to the field requires customised developments in solar technologies, appropriate investments in harnessing satellite technologies and empowering the illiterate by developing word processing programmes based on icon-forms. It also requires development banks to provide clear guidelines and electronic formats for loan applications and other forms of assistance rather than relying on the discretion and commitment of the desk officer to guide the client through the process. Transparency is a fundamental requirement for development home banking. Development home banking is an exciting new prospect which should command technical resources for its promotion within the development banking communities.

It is also important to keep in mind that while development organisations are pushing forward on the hardware and connectivity fronts, it will be important to temper enthusiasm for the potential of the new technology with the recognition that electronic communications by themselves can achieve little: they need to supplement open face-to-face communications, which in turn must take place within an appropriate framework of collaboration (Armstrong and Hagel, 1996). In particular, in establishing the conditions for dialogue – the common understanding of the activity's history, and the abandonment of the 'we-them' mentality in favour of the perspective of the unified 'us' – this initial foundation of trust and understanding will probably always have to be established on a face-to-face basis. In the same way that it is difficult to communicate by telephone with someone whom one has never met in person, but once one has met the person and established a face-to-face relationship, telephone conversation can be almost as close and intimate as face-to-face, and can continue the relationship at remote distances for long periods of time, so electronic communications are probably too impersonal for establishing the necessary foundation of trust that is crucial for substantive dialogue and effective business relationships.

The most likely roles for electronic mail and the Internet will be to make initial contacts, helping identify people with common interests, and to maintain and strengthen relationships that have already been made in person. Relationships based solely on electronic communication seem unlikely to be widespread: as with the telephone, until one meets face-to-face and in person, there is an underlying uncertainty between the participants that will make relationship always somewhat shaky. But once the initial foundation of trust is established or at least initiated, electronic communications can continue the relationship and build the trust to new levels, by maintaining communication links among people situated in many different geographical locations. It can help avoid misunderstandings, as the situation changes and new responses and actions are needed by different participants: electronic mail can keep everyone 'in the loop'. As new information emerges, any participant can easily inform all the others that the situation has changed and the new situation calls for different approaches from participants who might otherwise be uninformed either of the change in the situation or the need to change their behaviour. The electronic tools can in effect help create and maintain the shared understanding of a group committed to a common development purpose.

Establishing Electronic Communities: Linking up with African Expert Networks

Earlier we discussed the role that new technologies could play in connecting development agencies with African expertise: such linkages permit ready correction of project errors at each and every stage. We also indicated that the use of electronic communities among African clients and experts could play an important role in formulating key issues and identifying key problems which have to be addressed by development banks. In this section, we examine the prospect of organisational linkages between African experts and agency staff through electronic communities in more detail.

First, electronic communities can be established in ways which are not disruptive of organisational timetables but permit frequent and fast contact between participating individuals and organisations, thus providing the best opportunity for the appropriate modification and adjustment of the donor organisational processes and decisions to fit client needs. Dedicated electronic communities can be set up for particular projects or programmes and the membership of the community can be determined jointly between banker, clients and other affected interests. On-line participation is a practicable proposition which need not have the same delay characteristics as conventional participation arrangements.

Second, there is a need to develop and support independent African web sites and electronic fora where agendas are set by African perspectives (Spar and Bussgang, 1996). To give an example, the importance of the gender issue in African agriculture has often been overlooked by the development experts and decision-making. Both investors and technical specialists have thus bypassed the expertise and the centrality of the African woman in agriculture. An African gender web site could provide a location for African women to register and record their knowledge on the relationship between gender and agriculture in Africa, with the consequences that African women would acquire more confidence to press the relevance of their viewpoint and external experts would increasingly be obliged to pay attention to this cumulative knowledge base. Development agency support for organisations such as the Council for the Economic Empowerment of Women in Africa to establish web sites could do much to redress the existing imbalance between external experts and local experts which exists in agenda setting. It would have the important additional benefit of ensuring that African organisations are enabled to share information among themselves and correspondingly reduce the costs to themselves of gaining access to the data on their own circumstances – currently the best data on Africa is to be found outside Africa and is rarely accessible from Africa. The establishment of web sites is low cost activity with tremendous value-added in terms of information, education and communication benefits.

Thirdly, there is a need to ensure that development agency personnel make use of the expert information which is available to them through electronic fora. This requires some institutional provision for ensuring that development personnel have consulted with local experts and local sources of expertise on best practice in any relevant area of a project's operation In order for electronic fora to have their full impact, development agency personnel have to be educated not to sideline local expertise: one aspect of such education must be the up-skilling of development personnel in the new electronic forms.

Meeting the Future: The Importance of an Appropriate System Architecture

To conclude, appropriate thought must be given to the designing of organisational structures and processes for development banking which allow the client a greater access to information and a greater degree of control over the development process, while retaining the necessary transparency for the evaluation of both donor and client efficiency.

The prospects are promising. Already the World Bank under the leadership of its president, James D. Wolfensohn, has committed itself at the 1996 Annual Meeting to sharing its knowledge with clients and other stakeholders, and the preliminary steps to make this happen are already under way. USAID has also taken steps to support connectivity in Africa.

The electronic incorporation of client feedback in the interior of development organisations and support for the establishment of independent client web sites provide two simple but critical first steps towards the new emergent paradigm of micro-development banking. Bureaucracy has not generated either transparency or efficiency: new technology and new communications approaches can.

References and Background Reading

Armstrong, A. and Hagel III, J. (1996), 'The real value of on-line communities', *Harvard Business Review*, May/June, pp. 134–42.
Association of Women in Development Annual Conference, Meeting with James D. Wolfensohn, World Bank, Washington DC, 1966.

Burke, D. (1996), 'Virtual shopping; a breakthrough in marketing research', *Harvard Business Review*, March/April, pp. 120–33.

Cerny, K. (1996), 'Making local knowledge global', *Harvard Business Review*, May/June, pp. 22–41.

Ferlie, E. and Pettigrew, A. (1996), 'The nature and transformation of corporate headquarters: a review of recent literature and research agenda', *Journal of Management Studies*, 33:4, July, pp. 495–524.

Grieco, M.S. and Jones, P.M. (1994), 'A change in the policy climate? Current European perspectives on road pricing', *Urban Studies*.

Robertson, M., Swann, J. and Newell, S. (1996), 'The role of networks in the diffusion of technical innovation', *Journal of Management Studies*, 33:3, May, pp. 333–59.

Schein, E. (1996), 'Culture: the missing concept in organizational studies', *Administrative Science Quarterly*, 41:2, pp. 229–40.

Spar, D. and Bussgang, J.J. (1993), 'Ruling the net', *Harvard Business Review*, May/June, pp. 125–33.

Upton, D.M. and McAfee, A. (1996), 'The real virtual factory', *Harvard Business Review*, July/August, pp. 123–33.

Voices from African Women (1996), *Experts on our own development needs: participants in our future*, videotape, funded by the Swiss Trust Fund, administered by the World Bank and produced by the Centre for Social Policy Studies, University of Ghana, Legon.

Index

231

For Product Safety Concerns and Information please contact our EU
representative GPSR@taylorandfrancis.com Taylor & Francis Verlag GmbH,
Kaufingerstraße 24, 80331 München, Germany

Printed and bound by CPI Group (UK) Ltd, Croydon, CR0 4YY
08/06/2025
01896977-0013